CHURCHES NEVER TO BE FORGOTTEN

A GLIMPSE INTO THE SPIRITUAL LANDSCAPE OF HOWARD COUNTY, MARYLAND

PAINTINGS, PHOTOGRAPHY, PROSE AND POETRY BY

SHYAMI CODIPPILY

Foreword by Monsignor Anthony Sherman

The original Lisbon Church, Lisbon; 1883-1980

PAINTINGS, PHOTOGRAPHY, PROSE AND POETRY BY **SHYAMI CODIPPILY**

PHOTOGRAPHY OF PAINTINGS BY **CARMEN MALDONADO**

FOREWORD BY **MONSIGNOR ANTHONY SHERMAN;** EDITED BY **JUDY AND CLAIRE BOMAN**

COPYRIGHT 2009 SHYAMI CODIPPILY; ALL RIGHTS RESERVED. This book may not be reproduced in whole or in part, or transmitted in any form or by any means, electronic or mechanical, including photo-copying or recording, or by any information retrieval system without permission of Shyami Codippily.

COPYRIGHT MMIX BY SHYAMI CODIPPILY PAINTINGS: ALL RIGHTS RESERVED.
COPYRIGHT MMIX BY SHYAMI CODIPPILY PHOTOGRAPHY, PROSE AND POETRY: ALL RIGHTS RESERVED.

LIBRARY OF CONGRESS CONTROL NUMBER: 2009910576   ISBN: 1-43932-5351-X   EAN: 9781439253519

BOOKSURGE PUBLISHING
7290 B INVESTMENT DRIVE
NORTH CHARLESTON, SC 29418

AUTHOR CONTACT INFORMATION:
THE GALLERY AT MIRACLE MANOR, ATTN: SHYAMI CODIPPILY
3272 ROSEMARY LANE WEST FRIENDSHIP, MD 21794 USA
410-489-2875; www.shyami.com; shyami1@verizon.net

SUGGESTED RETAIL PRICE: US $19.95/ SOFT COVER; US $ 24.95/ HARD COVER   PRINTED IN USA

Present Lisbon United Methodist Church, Lisbon; 2008

ACKNOWLEDGEMENTS

I sincerely wish to thank all those who helped me to produce this book.

My husband Scott and son Taylor, my sister Deepthi, parents Hilarian and Sheila Codippily, and M.I.L. Mary Murphy, for much love and support. My art teacher Walter Bartman for many lessons.

Sr. Catherine Phelps, Msgr. Anthony Sherman, Fr. John Burkhard, Pastor Leslie Metcalf, Fr. Gerard Bowen, Pastor David Robinson, Rev. Rodney Ronneberg, Msgr. Joseph Luca, Fr. Noel Danielewicz, Rev. Jerry Cooper, Rev. Dina van Klaveren, Rev. Dr. Lisa Bandel-Sparks, Fr. Michael Ruane, Rev. Earl Mullins, Dr. Thomas Little and Fr. Matthew Buening who have provided me with much information and inspiration. Without their blessings, I could not have found the words to describe God's work.

My editors Judy and Claire Boman, and the photographer of my paintings - Carmen Maldonado, for their professionalism. BookSurge Publishing and their staff for their expertise.

Archivists J. E. Head, Cynthia McNaughten, Martha Embrey; the late Marguerite Sargent, Mary Warwick, Br. Fabrician; and many others for their dedication in recording church history. William Iager and Art Boone for accounts of their family history. Art Boone, David Jordan, and Rev. Bandel-Sparks for their generous photographs. The Howard County Historical Society for storing history.

Most of all, I wish to thank the past and present residents of Howard County, whose faith and dedication have enabled them to build their churches over the generations, and spread their generous spirits to those in need at home, and beyond the boundaries of this county.

FOREWORD

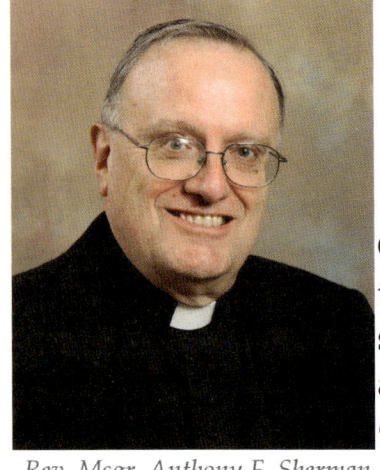

Rev. Msgr. Anthony F. Sherman

In her previous book, *Farms Never To Be Forgotten*, Shyami Codippily captured the impressive beauty of the landscapes of the many rustic farms of Howard County, Maryland. Moved by such tremendous beauty, it is no surprise that, with our hearts and minds having been lifted up, we would now be gifted with *Churches Never To Be Forgotten* as a sequel.

Part of the horizon of the culture of life in Howard County, Maryland, is the rich and diverse faith life of the people. The places where the Christian faith life of the people is expressed, nourished and celebrated are called churches. They are recognized as special places where we understand that God has loved us so much that we are moved to worshipful love in return.

Churches are significant to people in a number of diverse ways. For some, they are simply a landmark. They have always been part of the familiar setting in which people live and move. When suddenly the church is no longer where it has always been, there is a felt experience that something important has been lost. This deep sensitivity is expressed in the words of the title, *Never To Be Forgotten*.

There are those who recognize and cherish the fact that the church is the place where critical life moments of birth, sickness, suffering, life commitment, and death are experienced in a powerful and never to be forgotten way.

All of us eventually come to bear with our particular historical roots and the fact that we stand in relation to a bigger community than ourselves. Churches place us in contact not only with the history of the community in which they are located, but also in contact with a history and tradition that can go back thousands of years. On the basis of such a history, communities of faith then ask how they will contribute to the challenges of our own day and age.

As we experienced in *Farms Never To Be Forgotten*, our beings are so enriched whenever we can come into contact with the beauty around us. Churches as works of architecture can have an inherent beauty in themselves. There is a rich and diverse range of architectural styles but each, in its own way, can convey a sense of beauty to the human spirit. The very architecture of the building is able to lift up our hearts and minds.

Finally, for others, churches are those places where a welcoming community was found. That community supported and encouraged them on their life journey, and challenged them to realize that is only in service to others that we find a sense of fulfillment in life.

These are but a few of the significant meanings that churches have for people. As you page through this book, other reasons for the importance of churches may come to your mind. Whatever the reason that is most meaningful, take time to give thanks that you have been blessed with this gift of Divine love.

Reverend Monsignor Anthony F. Sherman
Executive Director
Secretariat of Divine Worship
United States Conference of Catholic Bishops

Corpus Christi Chapel, Ellicott City; 2008

CONTENTS

Foreword by Monsignor Anthony Sherman — Page 4

Why Church? by Father Michael Ruane — Page 7

Introduction — Page 8

Influence Of Church On Art & History — Page 9

Eastern Howard County — Page 10

Southern Howard County — Page 26

Central Howard County — Page 44

Western Howard County — Page 52

Northern Howard County — Page 72

Conclusion — Page 91

Sources Of Information & Inspiration — Page 93

Location Of Painting Sites & Churches — Page 94

Current Newspaper Headlines — Page 95

Franciscan Friary, Ellicott City; 2009

WHY CHURCH?

Church is where a congregation gathers at the local sanctuary on their spiritual journey home to the Father. It is through Jesus that we are at home with God. Our unity comes from Christ. <u>Ubi Christus, ibi ecclesia</u>. Where Christ is, there is the church. Here, at St. Michael's, there is a home and an extended family where the Spirit of Christ can dwell and where all who love Christ can meet in that Spirit.

Church is a sacred time and place where we grow in faith together, sing of the steadfast love of the Lord, and tell of His faithfulness to all generations. Church is a place where we find comfort, strength, and guidance; and grow in fellowship, discipleship and social conscience.

Christ is the Father's gift to us that must be unwrapped for another millennium, in the presence and power of the Holy Spirit. As His disciples in a modern age, we renew our Savior's vision of drawing all to Himself. We open wide the doors to Christ. By our faith, we bring others into Christ's healing presence.

Church is about relationships, past and present; about the old and the new; about our children, youth and adults. Church is about history, memories, an esprit de corps. It is about prayer and worship, evangelization, faith formation and enrichment, service, and stewardship. Church is about caring and sharing in ministry and activities, in hope and compassion.

We are the interlocking pieces of a jigsaw puzzle. Each year, as this puzzle is assembled, may it ever more clearly portray the face of Christ.

We are Catholic, universal, part of something bigger, beyond our parish boundaries, and even beyond our solar system.

Reverend Father Michael Ruane
Pastor, St. Michael's Roman Catholic Church
Poplar Springs, Maryland

Rev. Fr. Michael Ruane

St. Michael's Roman Catholic Church, Poplar Springs; 2007

INTRODUCTION

Howard County is located in the Central region of Maryland. It was formed in 1838, by the splitting of Anne Arundel County, and was officially recognized in 1851 by the Maryland General Assembly. It is named after John Edgar Howard, the fifth Governor of Maryland. According to the Howard County Economic Development Authority, presently, there are about 282,000 residents with a median income of $101,670, ranking third in the United States. Howard County is home to nationally recognized schools, thriving businesses, picturesque farms, and about 140 places of worship.

Among the many values that the residents hold dear is their faith in God. I came to this realization when I researched my first book, *Farms Never To Be Forgotten*. The long, hard days of farming began and ended with prayers to God for a rich harvest. During my experiences of producing this book, I discovered that throughout the county, people gather at their local church for blessings on their health, families, leaders, and community.

Churches Never To Be Forgotten is an exploratory journey through Howard County. As I traveled, painting and writing, my goal was to explore the history, mission, and dedication of the people associated with the churches that I had selected. My interviews with pastors and priests enlightened me on the teachings of religions, their denominations, and missions. During the process, I became aware that because of their spiritual connection with God, the clergy *and* the lay people were able to achieve amazing goals in their lives. Many churches were built with simple farm implements, manual labor, and a lot of heart, despite difficult economic conditions of the time.

This book includes fourteen oil paintings of fourteen churches, done over a period of fourteen months. Fourteen was an appropriate number because that is the number of Stations of the Cross that Christ experienced during His final days. The paintings were done in black, white, silver, pewter, blue-black, and charcoal gray. Painting in a limited palette was a challenge, as the nuances of light and shadow, perspective, and emotion had to be depicted without the dynamics of color. Interestingly, white and silver lent themselves to ethereal qualities. If the word "passionate" could describe the paintings in my farm book, I would say, "reflective" describes the paintings in this one.

Although there is no indication of the churches disappearing - unlike the farms - I put forth the title *Churches Never To Be Forgotten* with the meaning that we should never forget our need for daily reflection and spirituality. In a world that is rapidly changing, "Church" remains steadfast.

On a personal note, I would like to dedicate this book to the two sisters in my life. The first being my biological sister Deepthi, through whom I have gained a new perspective on the Divine, as I watch her struggle with her health. Perhaps it is my lesson to learn how humble I need to be, as I was given the gift of a healthy life. The other is Sister Catherine Phelps, of Trinity School. I have watched her unwavering dedication to God and His creation. She has guided me through her example of how to live in God's presence, and shown me how His work should never be forgotten.

INFLUENCE OF CHURCH ON ART & HISTORY

Dating back to the early dynasties of Egypt, around 3000 B.C., honoring a god or depicting scenes of the after-life were some of the reasons for humans to create visually. Examples can be seen in wall frescoes and earthenware, such as the "Palette Of King Narmer" from Hierakonpolis.

During the Middle Ages and the Renaissance, Christianity influenced most of European art. Without a doubt, Buddhism influenced Far Eastern art, and Islam influenced Middle Eastern art. Judaism, Hinduism and many tribal religions have also influenced many an artist to create works in places of worship and other public and private places.

A spiritual connection with the Divine is often a common thread among the great masters. Examples of Christian depiction from the Middle Ages can be seen in Otto's "Christ Washing The Feet Of Peter" from the year 1000, and Andrei Rublev's "Old Testament Trinity" from 1410.

During the Renaissance, there was an overwhelming production of art depicting Christian stories. One of the most inspirational books that I have read is *Michelangelo And The Pope's Ceiling* by Ross King, a biography about Michelangelo and his spirituality as he created his masterpieces for the Vatican in Rome. One could infer that God Himself guided each of Michelangelo's strokes as he painted the ceiling of the Sistine Chapel from 1509-1512, and carved each of his sculptures out of marble such as his "Pieta" from 1498-1499. Similarly, during the Baroque era, Rembrandt painted his "Jacob Blessing The Sons Of Joseph" in 1656; during the Impressionist era, Claude Monet painted many scenes of the Rouen Cathedral in the late 1890s; and during the Post Impressionist era, Gauguin painted "Vision After The Sermon" in 1888.

Since the Middle Ages, the Catholic Church has been documented as financially supporting some of the great masters. However, there were the woes of many, including Michelangelo, who had to jump through hoops to collect payment. One of the main reasons for the Church to commission religious or historical works was a way to teach most folk who were not literate at the time. The French Bayeux Tapestry from 1070, Da Vinci's "The Virgin Of The Rocks" from 1485, and Bosch's "Garden Of Delights" from 1500 are a few examples of the use of the power of art to convey a message.

How does the Church influence art and history today? In recent times, modern artists have been influenced in some form or fashion by religion. Barnett Newman's "The Stations Of The Cross" is a modern interpretation of Christ's final journey (if one could really see a cross in the black and white giant canvases). I can personally say that during my painting and writing journey of *Churches Never To Be Forgotten*, I have become more aware of the ecclesiastical accomplishments in Howard County alone, by those who have put God, or another superior being, first and foremost in their lives.

Whether a church be big or small, new or old, the architecture and interior designs that have been created by past and present generations have inspired me to capture visually and verbally the significance of these fourteen churches in Howard County, Maryland.

Eastern Howard County

Belmont Conference Center, Elkridge; Unity Baptist Church, Elkridge; Glenmar UMC, Ellicott City; OLPH Catholic Church, Ellicott City; 2009

Howard County's East is rich in history
Buildings are many along little greenery
Folk work hard, raise children, have fun
Their faith is as steady as the rising sun

As I traveled every day for the past eight years from the Western end of Howard County to the Eastern end, I noted the changes in the landscape. The fields of corn out West gave way to high density housing, shopping complexes, and multi-story office buildings as I headed East. Few of the churches (such as Melville Chapel) have been in existence before the founding of the county. Interestingly, one church - Glenmar United Methodist Church, which originated in 1954 - was rebuilt in 2008, in a very modern architectural style at a new location. Regardless of topographical appearance, religious denomination, or the architectural style of a church, I discovered that the deep reverence for God among those within a community is just as it was during the founding days.

Eastern Howard County is bounded by Baltimore County to the North, and Anne Arundel County to the South. Elkridge was once home to Caleb Dorsey, Jr. and his wife Pricilla. The Dorsey home, built in 1738, is now the Belmont Conference Center, a popular venue for conferences, weddings and special events. Elkridge, or Elks Landing as it was once known, is home to the Thomas Viaduct, the oldest stone bridge in the world, built in 1833, and named after Phillip E. Thomas, the first president of the B&O Railroad. Elkridge boasts its very own saint, Saint John Neumann, a pastor of St. Augustine Catholic Church, who preached there from 1849-1851. There are records of the Revolutionary War (1700s) and the Civil War (1800s) that went through this region. In recent times, the area has seen the addition of Timbers at Troy golf course, and many new businesses and homes.

Along my travels, I noticed that children, too, had a strong sense of a higher being, and exhibited wonderful ways of respecting God's creation. Many parochial schools in the area are proactive in religious education and participation. For example, at Trinity School in Eastern Ellicott City, Roman Catholicism is taught about twice a week in all the grades (pre-school - eighth grade), and many assemblies and church services are held to celebrate religious events and feasts throughout the year.

The churches that I have represented in this section with paintings, photographs, interviews, and history include Corpus Christi Chapel (Trinity School), Ellicott City; Melville Chapel United Methodist Church, Elkridge; and St. Augustine Catholic Church, Elkridge. Places and churches that I have represented with just photographs include the Belmont Conference Center, Unity Baptist Church, and roads leading to Baltimore, all in Elkridge; Glenmar UMC and Our Lady of Perpetual Help, both in Ellicott City. As I further explored these churches by painting and writing, I believed that there was much to be discovered beneath the hustle and bustle of Eastern Howard County.

"Lenten Light" 18"x18" o/c; March 2007

"LENTEN LIGHT"

(Corpus Christi Chapel, Ellicott City, MD)

Ash Wednesday is a solemn day in the Christian world. On this day, Jesus began His forty days in the wilderness (Lent), a time of sacrifice. During this time, Christ had to face many temptations and endure without food or drink. After the Last Supper, Jesus prayed at Mount Olivet, and on Good Friday, He journeyed through Jerusalem with a cross on His shoulders, upon which He was nailed.

In the present day, giving up a sugary treat such as chocolate for Lent, is a challenge for most, including myself. But, I knew that I would persevere, as I embarked on my new artistic and spiritual journey through Howard County, Maryland. The spiritual treats that I was about to experience was all that I needed to sustain myself throughout this project.

On the morning of February 21, 2007, I received my ashes from Sr. Catherine, following Mass at Corpus Christ Chapel at Trinity School, on Ilchester Road, in Ellicott City. Sister Catherine Phelps, principal and president at Trinity School, can be seen starting her day opening car doors during student arrival, performing administrative tasks, conducting classes, hosting coffees for parents and grandparents, and presiding at meetings during school hours and late into the night. Through her example, not only has she shaped her students, she has also shaped parents such as myself.

On Sunday, March 11, I completed "Lenten Light"- a black, white, and gray painting of Corpus Christi Chapel. While painting, I became akin to the soft light on the front of the building. The softness spoke of the emerging Spring, breaking away from the harshness of Winter. It also spoke of humility and reflection. As I painted "Lenten Light," I became one with nature and God, and enlightened in the meaning of Lent.

A year later, on February 6, 2008, I went to Corpus Christi Chapel again to receive my ashes. Mr. Rickbeil, the religion teacher at Trinity's Middle School, delivered his reflections on Ash Wednesday. He used a flashlight as his prop. He spoke about how the flashlight's three batteries resembled the three aspects of Lent: fasting, praying, and giving alms. He also spoke about when he first received a battery-charger, how thrilled he was to be able to re-charge his batteries, and how it symbolized our ability to re-charge our connection with God during this Lenten season. The Ash Wednesday service concluded with six 8th grade liturgical dancers performing a spiritual dance with lighted lamps.

For my husband and myself, this school was our first choice for our son Taylor to attend. We chose Corpus Christi Chapel as our place of worship for its unique architecture, beautiful interior, and small community. We have been attending service here now for eight years, and counting.

"Give thanks to the Lord because He is good; His love is eternal. Who can tell all the great things He has done? Who can praise Him enough?

Happy are those who obey His commands, who always do what is right..."

~Psalm 106

"My faith is very much nourished in how much I appreciate and receive back from the community."

~Fr. John Burkhard

Interior of Corpus Christi Chapel; 2007
Sister Catherine Phelps; 2009

Corpus Christi (Latin for Body of Christ) Chapel was erected in 1923. The official feast day of the chapel is Trinity Sunday, the Sunday after Pentecost. The chapel, originally known as Paine Hall of the Donaldson School, was constructed in the Elizabethan style of wood and stucco. The first floor housed a large auditorium with open fireplaces, and the second floor was the chapel, used as the center of religious life for the school.

The Donaldson school closed in 1933, due to financial difficulties, and in 1934, the Sisters of Notre Dame de Namur purchased the school and all its buildings for $40,000. Trinity School was founded by this order as an all girls' school, known as Trinity Preparatory School, and the Elementary School opened its doors in 1941. The newest building on campus is the state-of-the-art Middle School, built in 2002. Trinity's patron is Saint Julie Billiart, the foundress of the Sisters of Notre Dame de Namur.

On August 10, 1934, the Feast of St. Lawrence, the first Mass was celebrated in Corpus Christi Chapel. The celebrant was Rev. William Kerby, the chaplain of Trinity College, in Washington, D.C. The chapel has also been the place of choice for sisters to take their wows and celebrate their jubilees. The Trinity Sunday Community was formed in the early 1970s. Since then, families have come to the chapel for Mass, and it has been host to numerous baptisms, first communions, weddings, and funerals. Of significance are the Easter, Feast of Mary, Mother's Day, Father's Day, and Christmas celebrations. Since Trinity is not a parish church, it does not have a designated pastor. All the services are performed by visiting priests from other communities. Since 1997, Father John Burkhard has been celebrating Mass at Corpus Christi Chapel, as a volunteer from the Washington Theological Union. Aside from Sunday Mass, he also performs baptisms, and first communions at this chapel. Frequently, Monsignor Anthony Sherman celebrates Sunday Mass here, too.

Father Burkhard belonged to a parish in upstate New York before he moved to Washington, D.C. In comparison to his previous parish, he prefers a smaller parish such as the one at Trinity. Father Burkhard observed that people come here because they want to be here, and are supportive of one another. He noticed that there was a professionalism among the people and a commitment to the school - which he does not find in all places. This community, through its collections, reaches out to organizations such as the National Religious Retirement Fund and the Sisters' Academy.

Of his sermons, Father Burkhard said, "I try to deepen the real relationship and remind people of Christ's love for us, and our responsibilities as we try to deepen our spiritual lives." Of the first communions, Father Burkhard commented, "The way in which the children are prepared to grow up in their faith, and how their prayers are personally composed at the event, is very inspirational." Of the community as a whole, he reflected, "My faith is very much nourished in how much I appreciate and receive back from the community." His long-term goal for the Trinity Sunday Community is that it would grow, and that new families would feel comfortable being here.

I will never forget the inspirations I have received from Father Burkhard's sermons.

"Patience At Melville" 18"x18" o/c; March 2007

" PATIENCE AT MELVILLE"

(Melville Chapel United Methodist Church, Elkridge)

On the first day of Spring 2007, I drove into the adjoining town, Elkridge, looking for my next subject. I came across two small churches - one known as the First Baptist Church of Elkridge, and the other as Melville Chapel, about a block away. Anything with character always won me over, and a single glance at Melville Chapel had me hooked. The next day was Thursday, March 22, 2007, and I decided that was the day that I would paint Melville Chapel UMC in Elkridge, Maryland.

I arrived at the chapel at 8:45 a.m., after winding my way from a busy industrial Rte. 1 into the narrow streets of Elkridge, such as Furnace Avenue. The weatherman had called for warmth and sun, but it was chilly and overcast. "Be patient and have faith," whispered the scurrying squirrels. So, I set up and started to paint. The colossal oak tree in front of the chapel conveyed a sense of the "deep roots" of this community. The simplicity of the building's architecture gave a sense of sincerity to itself and what it held sacred. I continued to paint. It was now 9:15 a.m. Still, no sun. "Have patience and faith," whispered the gentle breeze as it blew around me. As I painted the arches of the windows and doors, and studied the curving branches of the oak tree, I was taken back to the time when this church was established. As a result, I felt compelled to include a few of the founders' tombstones that stood in the cemetery behind the church.

On the perimeter of the property was a white fence, and just beyond, one could see and hear the MARC (Maryland Rail Commuter) train which travels from Camden Yards in Baltimore to Union Station in Washington, D.C. Landmarks in Elkridge include the Thomas Viaduct, the Elkridge Furnace Inn, and Brumbaugh House, which was built in the late 1800s, and was once home of notable physicians including Dr. Brumbaugh.

Now it was 10:00 a.m. The sky slowly began to melt its clouds, and a glimmer of sun started to appear. Gradually, the sky transformed into the most translucent shade of cobalt blue. I paused to admire this transformed sky, and I was then reminded that God rewarded those who were patient.

I returned on Tuesday, March 27, to complete "Patience At Melville." Once again, at 10:00 a.m. the clouds parted, and the sun started to shine on the front of the chapel. The painting took on a life of its own now, as I identified the strongest areas of light to be between the great oak tree and the front entrance. To further emphasize the strong light, the tree and the left edge of the roof needed to be the darkest darks. The rest of the building and its surroundings were done in shades of blue-black, silver, pewter and charcoal gray.

As I painted the chapel, the hub-bub of traffic, trains, cars, and people seemed to fade into the background, and my patience continued to be rewarded with God's beauty.

"How clearly the sky reveals God's glory! How plainly it shows what He has done!

God made a home in the sky for the sun; it comes out in the morning like a happy bridegroom..."

~Psalm 19

"When hurricane Katrina hit New Orleans, this little congregation raised funds for the general relief in the area and for the Methodist ministers who were affected."

~Pstr. Leslie Metcalf

Melville Chapel United Methodist Church, Elkridge;
Roads and ramps leading from Elkridge to Baltimore; 2009

Melville Chapel United Methodist Church was begun in 1772 (four years before the Declaration of Independence), in the town known as Elk Ridge. It was founded by Francis Asbury, a circuit-rider who used to stop on the way North or South, to rest and preach in homes or school houses. In his diary, Mr. Asbury recalled the hospitality of many famous people who are still remembered today: Bruce, Worthington, Dorsey, and Pue. In 1784, Mr. Asbury was ordained as a Methodist bishop.

A board of trustees incorporated the church in 1834, by an act of the Maryland General Assembly. The origin of the name "Melville" is believed to be the name of another Methodist circuit rider, Melville B. Cox, who was described by his contemporaries as a "very promising, intelligent and lovely man, full of heroic Christian zeal."

After using several nearby sites for worship, in 1834, a brick church was built on its present location, but burned down in 1855. In 1885, a frame church building was built to replace the brick one. In the Fall of 1948, under the pastorate of Rev. Jacob Snyder, the capacity of the building was doubled. The board of trustees contracted to have the church moved forward upon a new concrete block foundation, and thereby formed a basement to accommodate the church school, the furnace room, kitchen, and restrooms.

"Brotherly Love" is what Pastor Leslie Metcalf is all about. When I stopped in to visit him on May 14, 2008, I found him in the basement kitchen of the chapel where he was busy marinating pork tenderloin for a dinner gathering of some of his parishioners, who were also his close friends. Pastor Metcalf was a retired minister who came to fill in for two weeks for the current pastor. Since that pastor sadly passed away, Pastor Metcalf was asked to take over, and has now been with Melville Chapel for seven years. He serves his parish with Sunday services, Bible studies, baptisms, weddings and funerals; and through his sermons, he tries to convey salvation through Jesus Christ. Of his many inspirational moments, Pastor Metcalf said, "When hurricane Katrina hit New Orleans in 2005, this little congregation of 219 members raised $40,000.00, of which $30,000.00 was used for general relief in the area, and $10,000.00 was used to help Methodist ministers who were affected."

In more recent times, the Carlyle Earp Memorial Fund, the Endowment Fund, and the Scholarship Fund have provided the financing for various projects within the church. One of their long term goals is soon to be fulfilled with the addition of a Fellowship Hall.

Of the many charities in which the church serves the community, foremost is the Elkridge Food Pantry, started by Mr. Herman Prehn and the local Kiwanis Club in 1996. The Clothing Ministry was later established by Pam Flynn in 2002, and in 2004, the two ministries joined to create the Elkridge Love Mission. The church extends itself overseas by supporting the U.S. troops in Iraq with supplies of food and necessities. The church also supports three children in Africa by providing for their education. Pastor Metcalf oversees these projects while fulfuilling the needs of his own congregation.

I will never forget the genuine interest Pastor Metcalf showed in his parishioners.

"Sunday Morning" 36"x36" o/c; April 2007

"SUNDAY MORNING"

(St. Augustine Catholic Church, Elkridge)

One day, while I was painting Melville Chapel, a delivery truck driver stopped by to chat. He said that I should visit the "Cathedral" just behind the railroad tracks. A cathedral in the middle of Elkridge? What next? I did not pay much attention to what he said at the time. But, a voice in the back of my head said that I should go take a look, anyway. I was glad that I did when I arrived at St. Augustine Catholic Church. Though not an official cathedral, it had the look and feel of one.

It was Monday, April 23, when I started painting St. Augustine's. The sky was a deep lapis blue. The front entrance was aglow as it was bathed in glorious morning sun. I set up my ailing easel at the edge of the cemetery on the church grounds. The three-quarter view of the church that I chose to paint proved to be quite challenging. In order for the front of the church to glow, I had to paint the side of the church in darker shades of gray. I stood in front of my easel from 8:45 a.m. - 10:30 a.m., trying to capture the essence of this massive church. When I got home later that morning, I took a look at my work. Because of the church's size, my perspective of it was completely off!

The next morning, I returned to a somewhat gray sky. But, that was fine, since I needed to correct all my mistakes in the linear perspective of "Sunday Morning." Painting buildings or any architectural structure was always a challenge for me, and my hopes were that with this project, the Divine and the dearly departed (I was positioned at the edge of the cemetery) would guide me through.

On Wednesday, April 25, I was once again rewarded for my efforts with a beautiful lapis blue sky - always an inspiration to paint. Lapis Lazuli is a deep blue stone that dates back to ancient Sumer, and can be seen in Sumerian sculptures around 2600 B.C. After the 12th century, it became widely used for making the pigment in Ultramarine blue paint. During the Renaissance period, Michelangelo saw its beauty and used it on the Sistine Chapel, from 1509-1512. He often had to trek to the next town to acquire it, since it was a scarce pigment.

When lapis blue is juxtaposed with a precious metal such as gold, they both vibrate with high intensity. Such intense color vibrations can be seen in the ornate ceiling of St. Augustine Church. Recently, the interior of the church was renovated, and the intricate carvings and paintings were cleaned - making the lapis blue and gold even more vibrant. The ceiling now sings louder of everything celestial!

When I witness such splendor, I often think of my sister and all those who are unable to have such experiences. Perhaps it is my job as an artist and writer to bring these experiences to them, in forms that could harness God's creation.

St. Augustine Catholic Church, Elkridge; 2007

Saint Augustine was born in Tagaste, North Africa, in the year 354 A.D. His mother was Saint Monica, whose wish was for her son to lead a Christian life. Augustine rejected the faith, and led a misguided life until he read the letters of Saint Paul. He then made up his mind to become a Christian, was baptized at 33, and gave all his worldly goods to the poor. He became a priest, and served as a bishop for 35 years. He died in 430 A.D. and his feast is celebrated on August 28.

Saint Augustine was an inspiration for the people in Elkridge, Maryland. In 1844, the cornerstone of the original church building was laid, and six months later, it was completed at the cost of $2,200.00. The present church was erected in 1901, and dedicated in 1902, by Cardinal Gibbons.

In 1944, to celebrate their Centennial Anniversary, church historian Mary Warwick wrote, "Yes, Elk Ridge Landing was a place of importance and renown, a place sufficiently well-established for the Holy Sacrifice of the Mass to be offered in its homes long before it was first celebrated in Baltimore... In Colonial times, our hillside saw procession of settlers on their way Northward and it looked down upon the commerce of that day, even as it does now. During the Revolution, there passed the equivalent of our present day troops carrying men and ammunition to the Continental Army in New York and New Jersey... Our Furnace Avenue of today bears the name as well as the remnants of a furnace in which was forged the liberty for which our armed forces fought..."

Of the many beautiful features of St. Augustine Church are the stained-glass windows. They were made in Innsbruck, Austria, and each one tells a story. In window #3, Saint Augustine is depicted with his mother, Saint Monica. The window also shows a miter, bishop's hat, signifying Saint Augustine's position as a bishop. In another window, the Latin phrase, "Tolle Lege", meaning "Take and Read" appears. Saint Augustine was converted to the faith through the scriptures.

Of the bygone pastors, of particular significance is Saint John Neumann. He served the parish from September, 1849 to December, 1851. He was canonized on June 19, 1977, and his shrine was erected and dedicated in 1978. Current pastor, Rev. Father Gerard Bowen believes the pastor sets the tone for the parish. Rev. Bowen, appointed by Archbishop Keeler in 1994 to St. Augustine's, tries to be hospitable, welcoming, and affirming to his congregation. In his sermons, he teaches how to honor, sanctify, and worship God and serve one another. "People have a sense of a heavenly kingdom in this church," says Rev. Bowen, who is proud of the recent renovations done to the church interior, including the paintings on the ceiling. Financially, he feels that his congregation is very generous in supporting the Cardinal's Lenten Appeal, Hurricane Katrina (2005) victims, and local organizations such as PATH.

Stained-glass windows inside St. Augustine's; 2007

The Cemetery at St. Augustine Catholic Church, Elkridge; 2007

St. Augustine Parochial School is an integral part of the church. It was one of the very first in the Archdiocese of Baltimore, and was established in 1857. The students were first taught by lay teachers, and from 1892, by the Sisters of Notre Dame. In 1957, the present school building was erected, and the student body is now about 250 pupils. Its teaching is based on the Christian principle: to teach as Jesus did, and to love and respect the rights of all students. One of the long-term proposed projects by Rev. Bowen is to strengthen the school with a multi-purpose building, to be built on a half-acre lot which the church recently purchased. This building would be used as the meeting place for boy-scouts, girl-scouts, youth ministries, and educational programs.

Among the religious activities offered at the church are the Anointing of the Sick and Elderly, and the May Crowning celebration of Mary. Among the organizations and support programs are Senior Luncheons, Life Teen, Bereavement, Pre-Cana, P.R.E.P., Choir and Folk Music Ministries. Many such programs can be found in large churches around the county. It is through the leadership of the pastor, and the dedication of the parishioners, that makes these programs viable and sustainable.

Of his moments at St. Augustine's, Rev. Bowen was most touched at the huge turnout for his 30th Anniversary Celebration. "I am still in the clouds over it," he commented with a broad grin.

It was soon Sunday, April 29, 2007. I decided that I would finish "Sunday Morning." The sky was a deep lapis blue again. There was a slight breeze blowing. I arrived just before 9:00 a.m. There were several Masses held at St. Augustine's. Among them were the 9:15 a.m. Organ Mass, 10:45 a.m. Choir Mass, and others without music. As I painted, I wanted to capture the parishioners walking into church. It was interesting to see varying physiques dressed in their Sunday best. Including human figures in a painting always gives the viewer a sense of scale of the buildings and surrounding objects.

Soon it was 9:15 a.m., and the organ started up. From the edge of the graveyard, I paused to listen. The music was jubilant. Pipe organs in themselves gave music a new dimension - as though the heavens had opened up, and the angels were blowing their horns. I listened as I painted in this harmony. The music helped me to keep my focus on the upper front section of the church - the part that stretched skyward toward the heavens.

As I was standing beside the graves in the cemetery, I got the feeling that the dearly departed too, were uplifted by the beautiful organ music. I could envision them in a bygone era, arriving in horse and carriage or on foot to church; women dressed in long gowns with hats, and men in tailcoats. Perhaps the women of the mid 1800s would worry that I would catch pneumonia from being out in harsh weather; perhaps the men would advise that being a woman, I should not be out and about at all, doing men's work. I am sure, however, that they would approve of church work.

By 10:15 a.m., the Mass was over, and my painting was complete. I bid farewell to the dearly departed as I left St. Augustine's.

I will never forget the words of wisdom that the dearly departed seemed to whisper.

Southern Howard County

Historic Savage Mill Manor, Savage; Temple Isaiah, Fulton; Mt. Zion UM Church, Highland; Grace Church, Fulton; 2007

Heading South is quite a challenge
The traffic is a discordant melange
Truth and Meaning are along roads
That lead to houses of God's Words

    Southern Howard County is bounded by Prince George's County to the East and Montgomery County to the West. On a map, one would find major roads such as Rte. 1, Rte. 29, Rte. 216, Rte. 108, and Interstate 95 running through it. "Traffic" is what Rte. 1 is all about. Trucks, that carry merchandise of all sorts, are intermingled with commuter cars and motorcycles. Mini-marts are alongside office buildings, and a business shingle can be seen on buildings of various shapes and sizes. The neighborhoods along Rte. 1 are economically mixed. The Rte. 1 corridor has many new housing and business developments alongside smaller and older one-level homes and "Mom & Pop" cafes. The contrast of the old with the new adds to the discordance of the general area.

    Along Rte. 1 are many towns, including Savage. Savage Mill (a textile mill) was established in 1820, by Amos Williams and his brothers with money borrowed from Mr. John Savage. Water mills were used to power the machines to manufacture mostly cotton canvas. During the 1800s, the canvas was used to make sails for the clipper ships that sailed into Baltimore Harbor. During the Civil War, they made canvas for tents, cannon covers, and bags. Similarly, this mill supplied canvas cloth for both World Wars. Many of the original buildings still stand, and house fine galleries and shops.

    Another historic landmark is the Bollman Truss Railroad Bridge, built around 1850. It is located at the junction of Gorman Road and Foundry Street, spanning the Little Patuxent River. It is one of the only standing iron railroad bridges left in the United States.

    Many of the churches in this area have been in existence before any of the major highways or houses were built. The topography was essentially farmland, and presently, a distinct demarcation of farm into township can be seen in the town of Maple Lawn, at the intersection of Rtes. 216 and 29.

    Maple Lawn Farm (established in 1839), belonging to the Iager family, is one of the few farms left in the region. Maple Lawn Farm was originally 500 acres, and about five years ago, 200 acres of the farm were sold and developed into a new multi-purpose community (called Maple Lawn) with upscale homes and restaurants, and its own zip-code.

    The churches that I have represented in this section with paintings, photographs, interviews, and history include Countryside Fellowship Church, Savage; St. Paul's Lutheran Church, Fulton; and St. Louis Catholic Church, Clarksville. Places and churches that I have represented with just photographs include Historic Savage Mill Manor and the traffic along Rte. 1, Savage; Mt. Zion United Methodist Church, Highland; Temple Isaiah, Grace Church, and Maple Lawn Farm, all in Fulton.

"Savage Countryside" 14"x12" o/c; May 2007

"SAVAGE COUNTRYSIDE"

(Countryside Fellowship Church)

As I looked around the perimeter of Howard County, I tried to pick churches of various denominations, and of unique architectural characteristics. So, why would I pick a church that was non-denominational, and architecturally speaking, only had a simple structure with a few windows to boast?

A House of God, for one, is not described in any Biblical form as being one of embellishment. In fact, the word "Church" applies to the people, not the structure. According to the Ephesians, "Through Him, the whole structure is held together and grows into a temple sacred in the Lord; in Him, you also are being built together into a dwelling place of God in the Spirit" (Ch. 2, v. 21-22). So, a simple structure would suffice for simple beliefs.

As a church, Countryside ascribes to the classic doctrines of Christianity. Basic Christian beliefs such as, "The one true and living God created all and is sovereign over all. He has existed eternally in three persons: The Father, Son and Holy Spirit," are practiced in this church. This church also practices "Believer's Baptism," and communion is served each week.

As a non-denominational church, Countryside is independent of denominational ties, and does not answer to, or take direction from, a central ruling board. Pastor David Robinson preaches simple rules that are the foundation of Christianity, and encourages his congregation to live by them.

Countryside Fellowship Church was first known as Laurel Chapel, and was established on Easter Sunday, in 1987. The building that houses the church is about 137 years old. The sanctuary's cornerstone was laid in 1871, and was the first church built in Savage. The building is constructed of white oak timber and the foundation still stands on whole timbers. The founding congregation was Grace Methodist Episcopal Church.

In its early years, Countryside Fellowship Church met in local schools. The founding pastor, Dan Schmidt, approached Grace Church with the idea of sharing meeting space. The Grace Church pastor gave the church building to Countryside, debt free. After some restoration work, Countryside held its first service in the sanctuary on October 30, 1994. Since then, a second story to its annex was built (the first story was built by Grace in 1970).

So, why would this busy town have a church named "Countryside"? Well, back in the 1800s, Savage was also a farming town, and this was the countryside, compared to its bustling and industrialized neighbors, Baltimore and Washington, D.C.

"All human beings are like grass, and all their glory is like wild flowers. The grass withers, and the flowers fall, but the Word of the Lord remains forever."

~The First Letter from Peter

"I serve God by celebrating church services and teaching Sunday school...
I try to convey the truth of Scripture as it applies to our everyday lives."

~Pstr. David Robinson

Countryside Fellowship Church, Savage;
Traffic along Rte. 1, Savage; 2007

The spiritual leadership of Countryside is the responsibility of the elders who serve the congregation. Each year, they elect or confirm trustees who manage the financial and legal matters of the church. A Ministry Council, composed of people coordinating various church ministries, and a Pastoral Care Team, made up of those who lead small groups engaged in personal discipleship, rounds out the organizational structure of the church.

Pastor David Robinson is a young man who started out as a computer programmer in Seattle, Washington. With the inspiration of a couple of verses from Scripture, Pastor Robinson found his new calling. He serves God by celebrating church services and teaching Sunday school. In his sermons, he tries to convey the truth of Scripture as it applies to our everyday lives.

Countryside's congregation is geographically mixed, with twenty-five percent of the people coming from Savage, and the rest coming from surrounding areas. Pstr. Robinson celebrates Sunday services here, and participates in joint services with other denominations for special events. Countryside's youth band has performed in local gatherings, and another group has started a coffee house.

Pastor Robinson hopes to have a positive influence by helping the needy in the community. The church helps to support seven missionaries, in the United States and abroad, and gives money to the Laurel Pregnancy Center. Countryside also supports other service organizations in Howard County. Pastor Robinson would like to help people grow spiritually, and hopes, "To be the Church that God intended for this time and place; to do whatever Jesus calls us to do."

For this time and place, the town of Savage is thriving. Savage Mill, on the weekends, is bustling with eager shoppers. Fine diners find The Ram's Head Inn to be top notch, and collectors flock to unique stores such as Hands of Time, Out of Africa, and International Antiques & Home Design.

After a little shopping excursion, I returned to paint this church. I experienced some new challenges trying to capture the light and space, with a limited palette, on a smaller cross-shaped canvas. So, to build spatial qualities, I used stronger grays and black for the foreground, the softer pewter and silver in the middle ground, and blue-black mixed with a lot of white for the background sky.

I tried to find a repeating motif in my subject, such as windows, that helped to establish rhythm in the painting. Pointed arched windows were always more interesting than semi-circular arched or rectangular windows. Back in Roman times, the architecture of the day was all semi-circular arches. This style is best exemplified in the architecture of St. Peter's Basilica in Rome, that began the revival of the Roman Classics (Renaissance). In Gothic times, the pointed arch was first introduced by Abbot Suger, and can be seen in his remodel of the Royal Abbey Church of St. Denis, France. More elaborate examples are Notre Dame Cathedral, France; and Gloucester Cathedral, England. Although Countryside Fellowship Church is thousands of miles away from Europe, let us remember that the area's original settlers were from Europe, and that architectural motifs transcended in this fashion.

I will never forget the simplicity of "Countryside"- it spoke volumes of fellowship.

"St. Paul In Pasture" 36"x36" o/c; May 2007

"ST. PAUL IN PASTURE"

(St. Paul's Lutheran Church, Fulton)

It was May 22, 2007. A few miles up from the bustling business district of Rte. 1, I found myself at the intersection of Rte. 216 and Murphy Road in Fulton, Maryland. It was just two years ago that I was here painting "Got Milk!", depicting the cows of Maple Lawn Farm. Two-hundred of the five-hundred acres of the original farm were developed into the new Maple Lawn Community. Three-hundred acres, and additional adjoining acres to the farm, are still in tact, and the dairy production continues. The farm is also well known for its fresh turkeys.

As I stood across the street from the farm to paint St. Paul's Lutheran Church, I felt a sense of de'j`avous - with the smell of the cow pastures, the rippling pond, and the barns and silos just feet away from where I stood.

At about noon, the sun sat right above the church bell, illuminating it above all the rest of the buildings. Since the strongest light was up above, everything else below the bell had to be painted in decreasing intensity, as the light descended and brought to life the features of the buildings. As I kept painting, I noticed that the stone work on the front of the buildings also had an integrity of its own. Each stone, an unique piece in itself, spoke of both solidity and change during the past century.

Architecturally, the Gothic influence was predominant. The pointed arched stained-glass windows and the flying buttresses on either side of the church were strong indications of the Gothic style. The concept of the flying buttress originated in Paris in the architecture of Notre Dame Cathedral, begun in 1163. Originally, buttresses (arched bridges) were created on the exterior to support critical points of the structure, so that the interior would be free of bulky supports, and thus, enhance the ethereal qualities of a church's interior.

St. Paul's Lutheran Church was founded in 1870, by a group of people (mostly of German descent) who were meeting in each other's homes since the late 1860s. The original church was a small wooden structure, built in 1871. In order to build the present stone church, during the early 1930s, the men of the congregation excavated the basement adjacent to the wooden church with horse-drawn scoops, picks, and shovels. The ladies raised funds by serving over 800 turkey dinners; and fried chicken, ham, and oyster suppers. They also held strawberry festivals, and staged plays. Since the 1930s, several additions and renovations have been made to the present church.

The senior pastor at St. Paul's is Reverend Rodney L. Ronneberg, and the associate pastor is Reverend Cathy Ammlung. In addition to their theological degrees, both have degrees in science.

St. Paul's Church serves its community by helping the Grassroots Crisis Intervention Center, year-round. During Christmas, this church provides food baskets, gifts, and other goods for ten families with young children.

Stained-glass windows in St. Paul's Lutheran Church; 2008

It was May 28, 2007 - Memorial Day. As I stood painting St. Paul's, I reflected on those who had given their lives to serve in wars for the freedoms we enjoy today. War is a fact of life, and has been so throughout the ages. The Crusades were one of the bloodiest times in history - all in the name of spreading Christianity.

How did the Lutheran Church evolve? Lutheranism had its beginnings in 1517, when Martin Luther publicly called for the correction of errors in the Medieval Church. Luther was a pastor, professor, author, composer of hymns, and reformer. Today, there are over eight million Lutherans in the United States, and they share a common faith with other Christians. They accept the Bible as the true source of Christian love, guidance, and doctrine, and they profess the Apostles', Nicene, and Athanasian Creeds. Their spiritual road to salvation is very similar to other Christian denominations - it is a road through which the Holy Spirit works to help Christians grow in grace.

Along this road (Rte. 216), I noticed several churches less than a mile apart from each other. Why was this particular area so dense in churches? Was there some sort of rivalry among the citizens of Fulton that inspired them to establish their own congregation? Was this the way each denomination was going to make its mark on history, by being slightly uphill from its neighbor? Or, was Rte. 216 one of the most traveled roads from times past, and it just seemed like the logical place to build a church? In my research, I discovered that Rte. 216 *is* a well traveled road as it extends from Laurel in Prince George's County to the Southern tip of Howard County, within close proximity to Montgomery County. As for my other questions, I am still looking for good answers.

Someone with good answers to many other questions is my friend Kathy Mariano, who lives in this community and attends St. Paul's on occasion. Her values are based on the Christian faith, and it shows in everything she does and says. Whether it be in the manner in which she raises her sons, or the generous spirit she exhibits to her friends, neighbors, and those in need, her words and deeds are to be admired. So, it came as no surprise when she tooted a friendly "hello" as she drove by with her sons on this Memorial Day.

Kathy, Nicholas and Benjamin Mariano outside St. Paul's Lutheran Church, Fulton; 2009

Maple Lawn Farm, Fulton; 2008

As a lay person, my concept of a church was that it was a place of worship and a place to participate in social and spiritual activities. Little did I know that it was also a place where many business decisions had to be made.

When I first arrived at St. Paul's, the minister was in an all-day meeting. Did not the minister have to perform a service somewhere? What could he possibly be doing at a meeting? Through my interviews of the clergy, I discovered that they were actively involved in the daily financial operations, and in many charitable fund-raising activities, of the church. They were also involved in capital campaigns, such as adding on new church buildings, to serve the needs of their parochial community.

St. Paul's, for instance, was planning on adding solar panels for power, and updating their fixtures. They would like to renovate their front door, their stained-glass windows, and facilities. They would also like to re-seal the parking lot, renew the carpet in the chapel, and replace the air-conditioning in the church and parish hall. Much like the clergy of bygone eras, a minister or a priest has to spend much of his time conceiving the grand plan, finding architects, applying for permits, and supervising projects on a daily basis, alongside praying for Divine guidance in the entire operation.

May 29, 2007 - another perfect, sunny day! I was working steadily when an elderly lady drove up and came out of her car to chat. It so happened that on the first day I had arrived at the church, I stopped by the rectory to try to introduce myself to the minister. I spoke with his wife, who let me know that the minister was in a meeting, and directed me to the main church entrance. I had brought with me a copy of my book *Farms Never To Be Forgotten* to give the minister, but since he was occupied, I intended to give it to him later. I lay the book on the grass beside me while I painted, and unfortunately, I left it there when I was done. Having realized my forgetfulness, when I got home, I called the church. Once again, the minister and his staff were in a meeting, and my book was still out there.

Thank heavens for grounds-keepers. The elderly lady, who drove up, informed me that her husband, the church grounds-keeper, had picked up the book and taken good care of it, with the hopes of finding the rightful owner. I was so touched by their caring, that I asked the lady to keep the book - because in the Christian spirit, "one good turn deserves another!"

Saint Paul the Apostle (a Jew born in Tarsus) was known for doing good deeds unto others, even though he originally took part in persecutions of Christians. One day, he had a vision that led him to convert. From then on, he began preaching, founded several communities, and lived in Rome. His name, of Latin origin, means "small in stature and humble."

Soon after my chat with the humble grounds-keeper's wife, I completed "St. Paul In Pasture." As I was packing up, I ran into a slick talking business man, who made promises of promoting my farm book. Taken in by his hot air, I gave him a copy of the book. Regretfully, I have not heard from him in years. I would gladly give a dozen books to the grounds-keeper and his wife, any day!

I will never forget the juxtaposition of Farm and Church - both built by the same people.

"Picnic Day" 36"x36" o/c; June 2007

"PICNIC DAY"

(St. Louis Catholic Church, Clarksville)

It was Saturday, June 16, 2007, and it was my 17th Wedding Anniversary to my husband, Scott Murphy. So, when I drove into St. Louis' parking lot and saw a white bridal limousine parked outside, it brought back memories. I recalled not only my beautiful wedding day, the event, and my husband, but also the spiritual aspects of Holy Matrimony.

Wedding vows have been exchanged in many a place, but a church wedding has the added benefit of all things sacred. At St. Louis' palatial new church (dedicated on April 23, 2006), everything within its walls spoke of the Divine. When I attended Mass here the previous Sunday, I was truly impressed by its modern interior, and its exterior architecture that blended so well with the older church and buildings surrounding it. The interior of the new church consisted of an exquisite marble altar, magnificent stained-glass windows on each side of the church, open two-story space, and modern equipment such as an audio-visual system that included a movie screen. Now that the new church is complete, efforts are being directed toward building the community.

If "Modernism" describes the new church, "Romanesque" describes the older church (known as the Chapel) that was built in 1889. During this era, farming was the main profession of most parishioners, and Clarksville was known as the center of the political scene - it was called the "Paris of the South."

The church's patron, Saint Louis (1214-1270), was a beloved King of France, who led two crusades, including one to Africa. He was canonized in 1297, for his merciful ruling, and his dedication to God. He is known as the protector of Franciscan tertiaries, the Military Order of St. Louis, the French Academy, and those who work with their hands (carpenters, marble workers, hair-dressers).

The origins of St. Louis parish in Clarksville dates back to 1757, with its first location being at the chapel in Doughoregan Manor, home of Charles Carroll of Carrollton, a signer of the Declaration of Independence. The first pastor was Fr. Augustine Verot, a French Sulpician. From 1859-1890, the congregation gathered at the small chapel that they built on Ten Oaks Road - which is still standing.

Monsignor Joseph Luca has been serving as pastor at St. Louis since 1996. Msgr. Luca had previously been a member of Cardinal Keeler's staff, and served at the Catholic Center in Baltimore, Maryland. Msgr. Luca serves his parish by celebrating Sunday Mass, assisting people where they are spiritually in need, and by reaching out beyond the parish as far as Haiti. Because of the growth in housing in the area, between 1996 and 2009, the parish has grown from 2800 families to 4900 families.

As I painted, I took in the light that streamed from above onto the church roofs, and down the sides of the walls. Spatial relationships had to be carefully depicted in varying tones, and the rose windows became my unifying motif, as they were present on the old and the new church buildings.

St. Louis Catholic Church, Chapel (1889), Clarksville; 2009

Monsignor Luca tries to convey that faith in God is a relationship, and that God shows us His love through Jesus. Msgr. Luca finds his parish of 4900 families to be very well educated and situated in the most prosperous part of the county, which translates into the extreme generosity of his parish.

The outreach programs of the church are numerous. St. Louis supports about eleven parishes in Baltimore City through Catholic Charities and Catholic Relief Services. The parishioners actively support two sister parishes in Appalachia, and run two schools in Haiti. Volunteers from St. Louis' parish travel to visit the Haitian parishes, schools, and their communities. The volunteers help the Haitians by financially and physically making improvements to their poor living conditions.

During Mass in September of 2008, Msgr. Luca spoke of the horrific devastation that hurricanes Gustav and Ike had caused in Haiti: a few nuns and other members of a school were trapped in a building with rising water, starvation, death and disease at their feet. During Msgr. Luca's call for aid for the Haitians, I couldn't help but count my own blessings. How fortunate I was to have my family, friends, food, shelter, and many luxuries in life - when the only prayer of those Haitians was to stay afloat! May the Lord always keep my heart open to those in need.

Teaching the Lord's way of life has been part of the curriculum at St. Louis Catholic School since its founding. The school opened in October 1923, with 41 students in seven grades, originally taught by the Sisters of Divine Providence of Kentucky. Since 1996, Ms. Terry Weiss has been the principal, and at present, there are about 450 students in grades K-8. The school is known for its academic excellence and quality sports programs.

Painting buildings and architectural details have their limitations since they are more static than trees or people. The bridal party that I was hoping to include in my painting left through the opposite side of the church from where I was perched. My hopes of including some people in my painting were almost gone - but wait - what was this? A sign that advertised St. Louis' annual picnic, coming up the following Saturday, June 23...I'll be there!

St. Louis Chapel (1859), Ten Oaks Rd, Clarksville; 2009

Art Boone, 2nd row, center; Father Eagan, 3rd row, right; with Grades 6,7&8, St. Louis School, Clarksville; 1953

St. Louis, like many big churches, has a very active community, and people have been gathering here for the annual Clarksville Picnic since 1878. The atmosphere of the picnic was like that of a county fair. As I stood on my perch, I could see a booth that read "Games, Food, Tickets." There was food for every taste bud: pizza, hot dogs, burgers, and fried dough. The games for the children included a moonbounce, face painting, hammer pounding, fishing for prizes, duck pond, and more. For the adults, there were Christmas bazaar items, white elephant items, silent auctions, and raffles.

Although the parking was grid-locked, nothing could take away from this perfect, clear sky, 80-degree family bonding day that I enjoyed with my twelve-year-old son, Taylor. After I completed the painting, he and I devoured a hamburger, a slice of pizza, a Sprite, and our favorite dessert - fried dough drenched in confectioner's sugar. We sat upon bales of hay, and listened to Mr. Art Boone play in his bluegrass band - Southwestern Bluegrass.

I first met Mr. Boone at a political event for Mr. Jim Adams, who was running for county council. Since then, I have seen him at the Howard County Fair, private gatherings and other local venues.

During a recent fireside chat, Mr. Boone recalled his school days at St. Louis as a young boy. He began there at the age of ten, in the fourth grade, in 1949. In his time, as many as three grades were taught in one classroom, so that it was possible to hear the same lessons three years in a row. "I'd say that we got a pretty good education... We had Catechism first thing, every morning. We were taught history, geography, science, arithmetic, and we had spelling bees." Mr. Boone recalled how strict the nuns were, but also how compassionate they were toward the country kids. Since most of them could not afford the uniforms, they were allowed to wear their barn shoes if they chose. Mr. Boone recalled that beneath the wooden four-room school house was a hall in which folks gathered to enjoy bingo parties, or to sing to the piano music, or to watch or participate in a play on the stage.

Art Boone served as an altar boy at St. Louis - until he outgrew the vestments. He recalled serving during High Masses, First Fridays, and special events such as weddings - all which were in Latin.

Mr. Boone's parents owned a truck farm - where they sold fruit and vegetables from their roadside stand. They also had about 40 steers in their pasture. The farm, originally 87 acres, was purchased by his grandfather in 1923. The deed stated that the farm was from a Doughoregan Manor (home of Charles Carroll) plat, and the lawyer was James Clark, father of the late Senator Jim Clark. The names Carroll and Clark are synonymous with Howard County, Maryland.

In the 1950s, a dozen eggs or sugar corn was $.60, and a half bushel of tomatoes was $1.50. As a youngster, Art's job was to feed hay to the steers and clean the manure in the barn. For the church picnic, his family donated chickens, corn, tomatoes, and other goods that Father Eagan picked up at the farm. The tradition of donating food, and other items, for the church picnic is still carried on by dedicated parishioners, annually.

Art Boone is a wonderful living resource of bygone times!

I will never forget the perfect day I spent with my son at the Clarksville Picnic.

Central Howard County

Columbia Mall & Town Ctr., Columbia; Dar-Al-Taqwa Mosque, Ellicott City;
Beth Shalom Congregation, Columbia; Wilde Lake Interfaith Ctr., Columbia; 2009

In the epicenter of Howard County's hub
Are tall buildings, a mall and many a pub
Worship at a Mosque, Synagogue, or Friary
With those who walk grounds with a rosary

When people think of Central Howard County, Columbia Mall and Town Center come to mind. Columbia, Maryland is known as the nation's most successful Planned Community. It was originally developed by the Rouse Company in the early 1960s, on 14,100 acres of rural land. Columbia is now a city with more than 97,000 residents, 2500 businesses, more than 60,000 jobs, and a wide selection of social, cultural, educational, entertainment and recreational programs. In 2008, it was voted by CNNMoney.com as the 8th best place to live in the United States.

Columbia is home to Toby's Dinner Theatre, the Rouse Theatre, the Smith Theatre, and the Merriweather Post Pavillion. The Columbia Mall, movie theatres, and numerous restaurants are where most people congregate. Of Columbia's more famous restaurants, Clyde's, Victoria's, and The Iron Bridge Wine Company are my favorites.

About a half mile across the street from the Iron Bridge Wine Company, in Western Ellicott City, is Dar-Al-Taqwa, a modern Mosque. Not knowing much about the Islamic religion, I decided to peek inside, although there was no one around the premises. To my amazement, I found a foyer that had a collection of brochures, all describing their outreach programs, youth programs, and prayer events. These projects and activities were very much the same as in the Christian denominations I had researched, and I was pleased to learn how much there was in common.

The Beth Shalom Congregation in Columbia is active not only with Sabbath services, religious celebrations, educational programs, but also with interfaith and social action programs. Among the holidays celebrated are Rosh Hashanah, Yom Kippur, Sukkot, Purim, and Tu B'Shevat -that celebrates the fruit of trees, which have special significance in the Bible as symbols of God's bounty and beneficence.

Within the walls of the Wilde Lake Interfaith Center, St. John The Evangelist Church and St. John United Church perform their services and conduct their administrative operations.

The only church that I have represented in this section with a painting, photographs, interview, and history is the Shrine of St. Anthony at the Franciscan Friary, which is located right in the middle of the county, even though its address is Ellicott City. Although I live only four miles down the road from the Friary, I had always driven by, but had not explored it until I started writing my farm book. Places and churches that I have represented with just photographs include the Columbia Mall and Town Center, Columbia; Dar-Al-Taqwa Mosque, Ellicott City; Beth Shalom Congregation, Columbia; and the Wilde Lake Interfaith Center, Columbia.

"Mary Most Blessed" 30"x30" o/c; September 2007

"MARY MOST BLESSED"

(The Shrine of St. Anthony, Franciscan Friary, Ellicott City)

On Sunday, July 1, 2007, my husband, son, and I decided to attend the 11:15 a.m. Mass at St. Louis in Clarksville. To my surprise, Father Noel from the Franciscan Friary was the celebrant. Upon leaving the church, Father Noel (the director until mid 2009) recognized us by name - which was enough for me to choose the Franciscan Friary as my next location to paint.

Few people know that just five miles outside of Columbia Town Center, on the Western tip of Ellicott City, sits one of the most beautiful friaries. The Franciscan Friary in Ellicott City is perched on land that was originally owned by Charles Carroll, signer of the Declaration of Independence.

It was now mid September. So, why has it been so long since I painted? The best reason of all - a family visit. Aunt Hyacinth, from my home country Sri Lanka, arrived in July, and on the first Friday in August, I brought her here to visit the Friary. Since she had been to all the sights in Washington D.C. on previous visits, I decided that she needed to visit a church that was on a setting that exemplified all of God's creation.

I took her inside the Friary of Saint Joseph Cupertino which was built in 1931, designed after the original Franciscan Friary in Assisi, Italy. The main floor houses the Shrine of Saint Anthony. In 1998, a relic of Saint Anthony of Padua was given to the Shrine, here in Ellicott City, by the Friars in Padua, Italy. The second floor houses the Friars' residences.

The Friars celebrate Mass here every weekday at noon. My aunt was impressed with the Renaissance style architecture and interior decor, including the wooden paneling and seating. The altar was unique - it incorporated a tree-trunk base representing Christ and four branches noting that all Christians, particularly Franciscans, follow Christ in the way of the Gospel. The shape of the altar was a butcher's block - a table of sacrifice and sacrament.

The Mass lasted about a half hour. After Mass, Aunt Hyacinth and I sat on a bench in front of the beautiful garden that included Saint Francis, the patron saint of animals. The grotto behind the garden included Saint Bernadette kneeling in front of Our Lady of Lourdes (Mary). I watched the early afternoon light flicker through the leaves, and I listened to the flowing water of the little water-fall at the edge of the grotto. My aunt and I ate our lunch here and reflected on life and all its intricacies.

The Blessed Virgin, Mary, is highly revered not only as the Mother of Jesus, but also for healing the sick and giving strength to those who seek her help. As I sat, I prayed to Mary for my sister's health, and for all those who help to take care of her.

Courtyard at the Franciscan Friary, Ellicott City; 2008

In 1700, Charles Carroll Sr. was granted 10,000 acres in Howard County (by Charles Calvert, the third Lord Baltimore), and he built Doughoregan Manor, his family estate, near what is now Folly Quarter Road. In 1776, Charles Carroll III signed the Declaration of Independence. In the early 1830s, Carroll III bequeathed a 1000 acre quadrant (soon called "Folly Quarter") to his grand-daughter Emily Caton MacTavish, where a smaller mansion was built - known as the Manor House. Upon his death in 1832, Carroll was buried in the chapel at Doughoregan Manor. The property went through many owners, and in 1928, Mr. Van Lear Black sold some of it to the Franciscan Friars.

The Companions of St. Anthony are people in mutual accompaniment, celebrating God's love as embodied in Saint Anthony of Padua. Father Vincent (who is the new director) and the Friars seek to promote the values that St. Anthony held so dear: Love for the Lord in the Eucharist; Knowledge of Scripture; Reconciliation and Penance as part of the Christian Journey; Opportunities for Christian Giving; Prayer; and Devotion to the Blessed Virgin Mary, the Mother of Jesus.

The Friars provide much for their visitors. They celebrate daily Mass at noon in the Shrine, and offer a special "Healing Mass" on the last Sunday of every month. The Friars take groups of people to Assisi on pilgrimages, host numerous gatherings (Crab Feasts, Concerts Under The Arches), and conduct a beautiful Renaissance style Midnight Mass on Christmas Eve. This Mass transports one to a bygone era with its flautist, choir, and poetry readers. The many nativities and religious displays are "sights to behold" within the Shrine and Friary. To usher in the New Year, in 2009, there was a reconciliatory Mass and breakfast.

The Manor House, now belonging to the Friary, is where various organizations like ChristLife and the Knights of Columbus conduct their meetings. The Knights of Columbus is a charitable organization that raises money for several projects in the community. One way that they raise money is by hosting an annual 10K race, that begins and ends on the Friary grounds. I participated in it on August 30, 2008, almost a year after I painted "Mary Most Blessed."

Just the other day, after chatting with Father Noel, I walked in one of the seven prayer paths entitled "LaVerna Trail." The woods, the colorful leaves, and the stations that were marked with a cross on significant trees, made it a joyous and reflective walk. The trail eventually opened up into the lush acres of cornfields at the bottom of the Franciscan Friary grounds.

A Station of the Cross along "LaVerna Trail"; 2008

Taylor Murphy at the Our Lady of Lourdes Grotto, Franciscan Friary, Ellicott City; 2007

I arrived at the Our Lady of Lourdes Grotto at 10:00 a.m., on September 14, 2007, after driving along the beautiful long driveway leading up to the Friary. The red canna lilies were still blooming in the garden in front of the grotto. The garden was bordered with large stones and filled with flowering plants. Saint Francis, the patron saint of animals, was depicted holding a dove in his hands and had a snake coiled around his neck. Behind Saint Francis were marble steps that lead up to the grotto's altar. A statue of a kneeling Saint Bernadette was on the left, and a statue of Mary stood at the top right of the stone grotto. The sky was mostly cloudy that day, and the wind was at an even pace. The surrounding trees and foliage were taking on the look of Fall.

On the following day, I returned to paint. The sun was shining, and the Blessed Virgin was bathed in its light. The sky was clear, amid a gusting breeze. Painting on this day was musical, because the wind made the hanging outdoor chimes create the most beautiful music that accompanied the songs of the birds. This beautiful day inspired me to title the painting "Mary Most Blessed." Saint Francis seemed to smile through all this splendor, too.

Saint Francis is honored with his own feast, and with the blessing of animals, in early October, in churches world wide. Saint Francis was born to a merchant in Assisi, Italy in 1181. After a vision, he gave up his worldly goods and dreams of becoming a soldier, to follow God in poverty. In 1209, he began preaching penitence, and lived on the goodwill of others. He was soon joined by his first companions, and founded the order of Friars Minor. In 1224, he received the stigmata. He died on October 3, 1226, and was canonized in 1228. Saint Francis is also known as the protector of merchants, rope-makers, ecologist, florists, traders, upholsterers, and poets.

During this series of black, white, and gray paintings, I have to say that I have grown from cautious brush-strokes in the early works to strokes of gradual confidence, and now, to strokes that have become alive with texture, in addition to strong contrasts and subtle nuances.

About a week later, I came back to complete my painting. This time, the church grounds-keeper was watering the plants. How lovely was her work - to keep the plants nourished and the beds tidy. I imagined Saint Francis watching her as she made her way around. I decided to incorporate her into the painting. While I was painting the grounds-keeper, I felt a strong kinship with Vincent van Gogh. Not only did I admire everything about his work, but I also admired the humility and respect he showed for nature, as he painted his subjects.

Vincent van Gogh loved the pastoral countryside, and all those who worked on the land. In a letter to his brother Theo (April 30, 1885), he spoke of the differences in painting a lady v. a peasant girl: I think a peasant girl is more beautiful than a lady, in her dusty, patched blue skirt and bodice, which get the most delicate hues from weather, wind, and sun... Although the grounds-keeper in my painting was not a peasant girl, her presence in the landscape was beautiful!

I will never forget Mary's glow as she listened to those who prayed to her.

Western Howard County

Glenwood Community Center, Glenwood; Glenelg United Methodist Church, Glenelg; Shepherd of the Glen Lutheran Church, Glenwood; Full Gospel Baptist Church, Cooksville; 2009

The West is where the crops still grow
Where the farmers still plough and mow
Love for God and country will always show
In all they do for those above and below

Western Howard County is bounded by Frederick, Carroll, and Montgomery counties. It is comprised of West Friendship, Glenelg, Glenwood, Cooksville, Woodbine, Lisbon, Poplar Springs, and Mt. Airy, to name a few towns. Some of the landmarks include the Howard County Fairgrounds, the Farm Heritage Museum, and the Glenwood Community Center, Senior Center, and Library.

This area is the most picturesque part of Howard County, with its rolling hills and pastures that are dotted with cows and silos. The sprawling fields that touch the big open sky are always a sight to behold. The ethic of hard work and general respect the residents have for one-another exemplify the teachings of religion. Although the area is transitioning from a farming community to that of a residential one, the values that were near and dear to the farmers are still apparent.

About three years ago, I made a presentation of my book *Farms Never To Be Forgotten*, to the Farm Bureau. Although I was the guest of honor, I was the one honored to be there. The board members started their morning with a blessing, a fully cooked breakfast, and then, the business of the day. Although I was there to talk about my experiences as a landscape painter and my analysis of the changes that were taking place, I was humbled to be talking to folks who lived on, and worked this land, daily. They prayed at sunrise and sunset, for a good yield, and the strength to handle the many challenges of weather, pests, and economic conditions.

There are many churches in the West that have an incredible heritage, but due to the limitations of this book, I am unable to incorporate them all. One church however, does deserve mention, and that is Glenelg United Methodist Church. GUMC began on Triadelphia Road as Westwood Chapel Methodist Episcopal Church, named after Rev. H.C. Westwood, in 1859. In 1889, the church moved to the corner of Triadelphia and Sharp Roads. The present church is located on Burntwoods Road, where worship services have taken place since 1970. GUMC's mission continues with much energy.

The churches I have represented in this section with paintings, photographs, interviews, and history include Gethsemane Baptist Church and St. Andrew's Episcopal Church at Union Chapel, Glenwood; Lisbon United Methodist Church, Lisbon; and St. Michael's Catholic Church, Poplar Springs. Places and churches I have represented with just photographs include the Glenwood Community Center, Walnut Springs Nursery, and Shepherd of the Glen Lutheran Church, Glenwood; Glenelg United Methodist Church, Glenelg; and Full Gospel Baptist Church, Cooksville.

54

"Simple Gethsemane" 24"x24" o/c; September 2007

"SIMPLE GETHSEMANE"

(Gethsemane Baptist Church, Glenwood)

Small churches can be just as interesting and beautiful as large, architecturally complex churches. Gethsemane Baptist Church's one-level simple building, with a large cross on the front of it, spoke volumes. It spoke of a community's reflective place to worship every Sunday. It also spoke of the humility that the Lord wishes for us to embrace.

The compositional emphasis here was on using the shapes within the building to fit on the canvas space, in a dimensionally interesting fashion. The church's steeple was the focus of this painting, and the area of strongest light. What was the purpose of a steeple? Was it an avenue by which to reach out to the heavens? Or, was it a method by which to channel the Divine Light into the church?

Rhythm is an element in art that is often overlooked in research and education. Rhythm is created by a repeating object, line, or color in increasing/decreasing size, shape, or intensity.

Throughout the history of Modern Art, one can see examples of the use of rhythm in works by artists such as Giorgio de Chirico with his "Mystery And Melancholy Of A Street," 1914; Edward Hopper with his "Early Sunday Morning," 1930; and Frank Stella with his "Empress Of India," 1965.

In "Simple Gethsemane," I have painted the church windows on the side of the building going from right to left in decreasing order, as the building receded from right to left. Also, I have painted repeating vertical lines such as the columns on the front of the building, and repeating triangular shapes within the steeple and roof line. To balance out the geometric repetition, I have painted the foreground tree and its branches with curving lines, as it was undulating in the Autumn breeze.

Autumn is the most colorful time of year. An abundance of color can be found at the Walnut Springs Nursery, just down the road from Gethsemane. Mr. J. Alvin Smith, who founded Walnut Springs in 1964, began as an ornamental grower. While in high school, he began to work part time for the Department of Agriculture, where he worked as a research associate in Plant Genetics. Smith's award winning company now supplies ornamentals, rhododendrons, foliage, poinsettia and annuals to garden centers and landscape contractors in Baltimore, Washington, D.C., and Northern Virginia. His beautiful flowers and shrubs also adorn the Capitol and the White House gardens.

Across the way on Rte. 97 is "Longwood House," a manor built in 1818, and purchased by Mr. Al Smith for his son and daughter-in-law. This manor originally belonged to Dr. Gustavus Warfield. About five years ago, it was on display as a "Decorator Show House," put on by Historic Ellicott City. When I visited it, I was awed at the expanse of house, and grounds (99 acres). An attached cottage housed the doctor's office with his tools and supplies in tact. Dr. Warfield saw patients regularly, and sometimes kept them for observation in a second-story room that had a few beds. This became the area's first hospital. The manor has been renovated, and is now a beautiful, modernized home.

"The Lord is my Shepherd; I have everything I need. He lets me rest in fields of green grass and leads me to quiet pools of fresh water... He gives me new strength..."

~Psalm 23

"The people of my congregation are most loving and teachable and encouraging...They assist those in need, counsel inmates and lead worship services..."

~Pstr. Jerry Cooper

Gethsemane Baptist Church, Glenwood; 2008
Mr. J. A. Smith, Walnut Springs Nursery, Glenwood; 2009

Gethsemane Baptist Church was founded in May, 1978. The first congregation of 43 members met at the home of Rev. Eugene Brotherton. The church was named "Gethsemane" after the garden at the foot of Mount Olivet in Jerusalem, most documented as the place in which Christ prayed after the Last Supper. In 1984, four acres of land on Burntwoods Road, Glenwood, were given to Gethsemane Baptist Church by the Baptist Convention of Maryland/Delaware. The church raised over $100,000.00 to construct its current building - begun in September 1984, and dedicated on June 30, 1985. During the mid 1990s, the church acquired an additional four acres, and a house - that is now home to the church's Sunday school, youth groups, and the pastor. The main building is also home to the Gethsemane Korean Baptist Church.

During the year 2000, more funds were raised to expand and renovate the church building. In 2002, a beautiful new facility was completed. In September, 2002, Pastor Jerry Cooper became, and still is, the pastor of Gethsemane Baptist Church. He is assisted by Rob Stephens, Andy Honeycut, and my neighbor Mike Parker.

While I was painting, Pastor Cooper saw me and asked me what I was doing. He seemed genuinely pleased about my project. Although I could not interview him in person, I was able to connect with him via e-mail. The response I received was very touching.

As a man of God, Pastor Cooper serves his church family by praying for the people, visiting them, and teaching them the Bible and how it applies to their lives. On a practical level, he offers them handyman skills, and leads them on mission trips to other countries.

In his sermons, he seeks to accurately interpret God's Word (the Bible), clearly explain what it says, and give applications to daily life as he makes the message interesting and relevant.

Of his congregation, Pastor Cooper said that the people of Gethsemane Baptist were the most loving and teachable, and encouraging of the four churches that he had served since 1982.

Under Pastor Cooper 's leadership, the congregation is very involved within the community. They give free English classes to immigrants, material assistance to people in need, volunteer in local public schools, counsel inmates, and lead worship services at the Howard County Detention Center, and much more. Gethsemane Baptist Church's charitable organizations include the Liberty Learning Center, Laurel Pregnancy Center, and the Christian Jail Ministry.

In the future, Pastor Cooper would like to offer multiple worship services. He would like to multiply small groups that meet in homes to worship, pray, and study the Bible, so that families could be equipped to practice their faith at home. Pastor Cooper and his missionaries have also been inspired to adopt Antigua and Barbuda, and to share the Gospel with all the people there, and to start churches that would give birth to more churches. They have been inspired to be the missionaries for the purpose of sharing the Good News about Jesus with everybody.

I will never forget the simplicity within Gethsemane and the history within its vicinity.

"Memorial Bell" 14"x12" o/c; October 2007

"MEMORIAL BELL"

(St. Andrew's Episcopal Church at the Union Chapel, Glenwood)

It was now October, 2007. The leaves had started to turn color and the air was filled with the scents of Fall. Painting St. Andrew's at the Union Chapel was charming. The aroma of boxwood was the first thing that I experienced when I stepped out of my car. As I painted the chapel, I was enthralled with the soft light that dappled on the front of the building. It was telling of the season, and it brought a sense of urgency to paint before gusting winds and wintery weather approached.

Glenwood is the rising new hub of Western Howard County. St. Andrew's is located on Rte. 97, within a mile of the Glenwood Library and the Glenwood Community Center and Senior Center. Rte. 97 has become the most traveled alternate route, from Baltimore to Washington, D.C., as the other major highways, such as Rte. 95 and Rte. 29, have become grid-locked during rush-hour.

As a rising hub, Glenwood has several new housing developments, and two shopping-strips across the street from each other on Rte. 97. One can find a beauty parlor, auto repair shop, packaging and shipping store, and a gourmet food store on one side of the street; a book store, veterinary clinic, liquor store, and an authentic Italian restaurant named Vesuvio's (my favorite) on the other side of the street.

During my explorations, I came to realize that the history of a place is not confined to its four walls. It often extends to its immediate surroundings, and beyond. Frequently, the beginnings of a place is the result of one person or a small group of people from different locations and walks of life, coming together with one mission, and inspiring in others the purpose of that mission.

One inspired member was Cynthia McNaughten. During the summer of 1981, Cinny was driving from her home in Rockville, Maryland, through Olney along Rte. 97, headed North to Gettysburg, during a torrential storm. She saw a sign on the front lawn of St. Andrew's at the Union Chapel. She came back the next day to visit the church, and found out that it was an extremely active congregation that was barely a year old. Although the chapel did not have any running water or bathroom facilities other than an out-house, Cinny liked what she saw, and has been a member of St. Andrew's ever since. She is now actively organizing the church's archives. Despite her busy schedule, she took the time to gather historic information for my project - a gesture of a generous spirit.

St. Andrew's pastor - Reverend Dina van Klaveren, the members of St. Andrew's board of trustees, and parishioners, including Cinny, spend countless hours dedicating their time and efforts to the mission of their church.

Dedication is what elevates the chosen few into the realm of saint-hood. Saint Andrew was the brother of Simon Peter. They were both fishermen at Capernaum. A disciple of John the Baptist, Andrew was one of the first to follow Jesus. His cult was especially popular during the Middle Ages. He is the protector of fishermen, fishmongers and paralytics.

"The world and all that is in it belong to the Lord; the earth and all who live on it are His...

Fling wide the gates, open the ancient doors, and the great King will come in..."

~Psalm 24

"St. Andrew's has partnered with the Church of the Guardian Angel in Baltimore, MD, in their missionary goals. Several members of the congregation deliver baskets of food, and spend time with the needy in helping them do projects and tasks of daily life."

~Rev. Dina van Klaveren

Interior of, and the bell at St. Andrew's, Union Chapel, Glenwood; 2008

The origins of the Union Chapel go back to 1833, when the land for the building was given by a Deed of Trust, by Charles D. Warfield. Aside from being used as a Methodist meeting house at the time, it was also used for cavalry and foot soldier training, and for mustering Union troops during the Civil War, around 1863. St. Andrew's is linked to Mt. Carmel, the original Episcopal Church, located ten miles south of Glenwood, at the intersection of Rte. 97 and New Hampshire Avenue.

The founders of St. Andrew's started to meet at Glenwood Middle School while Union Chapel was being renovated. A matching fund grant from the Maryland Historical Trust provided the initial funding to begin restoration in 1977. Much of the painting and refurbishing was done by the trustees, and neighbors and friends of Union Chapel, from the Glenwood-Cooksville communities. After the restoration, St. Andrew's celebrated its first service in the new Union Chapel on Christmas Eve, 1980.

As the congregation grew, so did their needs. With the generous donation of funds from Mrs. Adelaide C. Riggs, an extension was built in 1994. The extension includes a Sunday school meeting space, bathrooms, greeting area, pastor's office, and kitchen. Though sufficient at the time, the congregation grew bigger, and needed more space. So, St. Andrew's built an entire new Parish House a block away from the Union Chapel, with money for the land gifted by Bill Pindell. The new Parish House (including full worship space, offices, and classrooms) was dedicated on January 26, 2003.

When I stopped by one day to visit the Union Chapel, I was attracted at first to the bell that stood along the walkway leading up to the steps of the front entrance. I later found out that the bell was given to St. Andrew's in memory of Robert P. Bays, Jr. by the Bird and Bays families in 1988. The great oak tree that stands on the front lawn has a significant story, too. It was a sapling from the great Wye Oak that stood tall on the Eastern Shore, and had since come down during a storm in 2002. The sapling was planted on Arbor Day in 1976, instrumented by Mrs. Marguerite Ridgely (Mrs. Warren) Sargent and the Cattail River Garden Club. Mrs. Sargent served as Chapel Historian until her death in 2008. Because of its picturesque front setting, Union Chapel has been the ideal location for baptisms, weddings, and funerals. If I were an infant, a newlywed, or one of the dearly departed, I would want to take in the sight of the October light that bathed the chapel, and the smell of boxwood that permeated the air around it, as I embarked on my journey.

St. Andrew's has partnered with the Church of the Guardian Angel in Baltimore, Maryland, in their missionary goals. Several members of the congregation deliver baskets of food, and spend time with the needy in helping them do projects and tasks of daily life. St. Andrew's also recently sent a group of people to Honduras, Appalachia, and New Orleans to help them improve their daily conditions.

As the Glenwood community grows, St. Andrew's continues to grow with purpose and activity. Cinny McNaughten hopes that her efforts, of organizing the church archives, will provide future generations with a church history that is treasured.

I will never forget the bell at St. Andrew's that stood steadfast in loving memory.

"Land And Sky United" 36"x36" o/c; October 2007

"LAND AND SKY UNITED"

(Lisbon United Methodist Church, Lisbon)

Moving farther West, I found myself in the little town of Lisbon. The Lisbon United Methodist Church struck my fancy not for its architecture, but for the land on which it sat. The wide, open space of its four acres gave way to the horizon and the rippling clouds in the heavens above. I had never been so excited before by a sky full of rippling clouds!

How does one paint rippling clouds, especially when their formations were different each day? For starters, I had to find the dark and light areas within the clouds, themselves. Figuring out the light and dark areas was always a challenge within any landscape, as the shadows changed as the day went by. The same applied to clouds, except that I not only had the sun's time-table, but I also had the wind's time-table with which to deal. On a windy day, those clouds were zooming by, and unfortunately, my paint-brush did not double up as a magic wand with which I could command them to be still. So, I had to rely on my visual memory to capture a cluster of clouds, as they appeared for one brief second, onto my canvas. When I came back on different days to paint, I would add a new cluster onto an area that I had not previously worked. In this manner, several days of cloud patterns appeared on my canvas. On the last day, there were an abundance of clusters and movement, and my hands and brush moved freely and vigorously across the canvas to unite all of them. Thus, the final product was accomplished.

Painting flat, open space had its own set of challenges. How could I make something interesting? The church, too, was situated 90-degrees from the open field that I was facing - a new discovery. So, on the right wing of my cross, I composed the church at a 45-degree angle. This enabled me to capture the church, the depth of its surrounding field, the playground, and the driveway of the church. Another challenge: the open field needed something to give it definition. As I looked closer, I could see shadows on it that were created by the clouds above. So, I captured them in varying shades of gray.

Another concept that an artist has to keep in mind, while painting, is the order of importance of the details within the subject. In this painting, the cross on the front of the church was the most significant element, and I featured it in sharp contrasts: a silvery- white cross on a black background. The rest of the elements - the steeple, the sheds, the trees, and the playground equipment - were done in less contrasts. Although the side of the steeple was where the strongest light was, I made it more subtle, so that the focus remained on the front cross of the church.

Though the challenges were many, especially when trying to paint on a day with gusting winds, one added bonus when painting God's creation was that I always felt like I was connected to Him. Even as a child, whenever I was painting, it was always a spiritual experience.

Interior of Lisbon United Methodist Church; 2008

The Lisbon United Methodist Church has many decades of long history. I have come to learn that much of church history was compiled through the intense dedication and labor of archivists. This church's history was written by Martha Embrey, Mary Slagle, Elizabeth Mullinix and several others.

When I came to interview Reverend Dr. Lisa Bandel-Sparks, the good pastor had also invited the church archivist, Martha Embrey. Mrs. Martha Embrey grew up in the Lisbon community, and her family has been part of the Lisbon church since its conception. She came from a farming background (her maiden name was Mullinix), and lives on Daisy Road, next to the Maple Dell Farm, owned by the Patrick family. She currently has a son in the Lisbon Fire Department.

According to the history compiled by Mrs. Embrey and her associates, in August, 1820, two lots were purchased for the sum of one dollar, to erect a building for the use of many denominations of Christianity to preach. There was a provision that stated that the Methodists would have one day, every two weeks, for the purpose of circuit preaching. The original structure was called "Free Stone Church," and it stood on the present location of the Lisbon Elementary School. In 1883, under the direction of Rev. James Cadden and Mr. Daniel Hartsock, the Lisbon Church, a Gothic structure (photo on page 2), was erected on the corner of Rte. 144 and Church Alley.

The Methodist Protestant, Methodist Episcopal North, and Methodist Episcopal South, united in 1939, and became the Methodist Church. Reverend Charles Subock was the pastor at the time. In 1962, Lisbon became an independent church with Orin Dooley as its first pastor. A parsonage was built on Daisy Road, in 1963. In January, 1967, a fire destroyed the education building, and the congregation moved into the Lisbon School, where Sunday school and worship services were held. A new education building was erected in 1970, under the leadership of Rev. Floyd Cooper.

In 1968, the Methodist and Evangelical United Brethren came together and formed the United Methodist Church. In 1976, the community celebrated Heritage Day with an old fashioned worship service. The pastor and his wife were brought to church in a horse drawn buggy. The congregation wore clothes of bygone days. After the service, they had a picnic lunch.

Construction for the present Lisbon United Methodist Church (photo on page 3) was begun in June, 1981, and the first service was held on December 20, 1981. It was a spiritual day.

"Spiritual" is a word that best describes the people of Lisbon. In December, 2007, I attended their "Breakfast with Santa," held at the firehouse. The firehouse was packed with the entire town to celebrate the season, and to take part in the large helpings of eggs, bacon, sausage, pancakes, grits, and a visit from Santa. Although I was a newcomer, everyone made me feel like I belonged there. They also showed reverence in everything they did and said, especially to their guest of honor, Sargent Little, who had recently returned from Iraq as a double amputee.

Sargent Little receiving his MD General Assembly award from Delegate Warren Miller at the "Breakfast with Santa," Lisbon Firehouse; 2007

Frank Penn, Kenneth Crosswhite, and Michael Mills of the Lisbon Volunteer Fire Department, Station 4, Lisbon; 2009

On October 30, 2007, I came to Lisbon to complete my painting. What should I see? On the front field were three equestrians atop their horses, getting ready to go for a mid-afternoon ride. The scene brought to mind the images of the circuit riders from the 1800s - who would ride into towns to preach the Word of God. It was a beautiful 75-degree day for it, too. The air was crisp, the sun in full shine, and for a landscape painter, it was a perfect "zen" day.

Others in the area felt the same way about the day, too: the owner of a convenience store (the only one for miles) had his bluegrass and '80s music blasting; motorcyclists were out and about, and were revving their engines; and a neighborhood dog was expressing his excitement, at all the activity, by barking his head off!

The Lisbon community is very strongly inter-connected, and the church provides not only for the spiritual needs, but also for the daily needs of the parishioners. On the lower level of the Lisbon United Methodist Church, a day care center was established to accommodate children of working families.

When I was writing my previous book, I had the honor of working with Dr. Allan Bandel, Professor Emeritus from the University of Maryland, and long-time resident of Western Howard County. Little did I realize then that I would be interviewing his niece, the Reverend Dr. Lisa Bandel-Sparks, who is the pastor of Lisbon United Methodist Church.

Reverend Dr. Lisa Bandel-Sparks finds this location very pleasing because of her family roots in the farming community. She began preaching here in July, 2002. She is also the chaplain for the Lisbon Firehouse and the entire county. She conducts various services and a special service for the firemen every year, on September 11, to honor those who gave their lives during the tragedies of September 11, 2001, in New York City, Washington D.C., and a field in Pennsylvania.

Every year, around the middle of May (for the past five years), Rev. Dr. Bandel-Sparks honors the farmers by conducting a special blessing for them. The farmers bring their tractors and other equipment to the church parking lot for her to pray over them for a healthy growing season, and a bountiful harvest. This is known as "Rogation Sunday." In a recent newspaper interview, of this event she said, "It is important to show the connection with the fields and the farm...the grain that is used in the making of bread and the grapes for the wine." This blessing draws a great crowd, as the area is still steeped in family farming.

When away from her immediate community, Rev. Dr. Bandel-Sparks can be seen networking with other communities. She has also participated in a television series hosted by the Horizon Foundation. For Rev. Dr. Bandel-Sparks, family ties and farming roots are the foundations of her church and community!

I will never forget the sincerity of Dr. Allan Bandel & his niece Rev. Dr. Lisa Bandel-Sparks.

"Where Are You Christmas?" 12"x14" o/c; November 2007

"WHERE ARE YOU CHRISTMAS?"

(St. Michael's Catholic Church, Poplar Springs)

It was now the end of November, 2007, and the holiday season was in the air. Traveling farther West in Howard County, I found myself in Poplar Springs. Poplar Springs is a little town just below Mt. Airy, the Western tip of Howard County. I had painted and written about Mt. Airy previously, and while traveling there, I had frequently driven by St. Michael's Road.

Along St. Michael's Road is a beautiful little church, St. Michael's Catholic Church. Small churches always have large appeal for me, and St. Michael's was no exception. I found lots of appeal in the 1:00 p.m. sunlight that dappled on the back of the church building, the grave stones, and the large oak tree in the foreground.

Whenever I was out painting, I was always happy to be in my own world, doing what pleased me most. However, to the passer-by, I was a thing out of the ordinary - something that landed in their realm of being, that was worthy of an investigation. (I can still recall a neighbor calling the police on me when I was painting on my parents' front lawn one night, while I was a high school student.) So, that was how I met Reverend Father Michael, of St. Michael's Catholic Church, on St. Michael's Road.

In his kind-hearted manner, Father Mike first asked me if everything was "O.K." He then asked me what I was doing, which I explained. I also shared with him my farm book. He told me that he had purchased a copy of it at the nearby convenience store. We ended our conversation with a hopeful future meeting to get a detailed history of the church.

It was soon Christmas Eve. I was in search all December for the true meaning of Christmas. I certainly did not find it in the shopping mall. I kept looking for it in the cookies I was baking, the cleaning chores I was doing to beautify my home, and in the traditions with which I had grown up. I was getting closer with each "thing" I did - but I was not there, yet. So, I decided to go looking for Christmas, and my travels took me back to St. Michael's Church. The same dappling afternoon sunlight greeted me.

As I stood taking a few photographs, Father Michael spotted me, and came out of the church to chat. Once again, I felt like I had been "caught" admiring God's creation. Father Mike asked me into the church, and he also invited me to visit the Nativity that was outside the new Church Activities Building, across the street. I followed his instructions, and to my amazement, found the most beautiful Nativity scene, that was brightly illuminated by the afternoon sun. I had found Christmas! This was how it all began, and this was what priests and other clergy members wanted people to see and know. After taking a few more photographs, I headed home, my heart filled with joy, as I then knew that I was ready to truly celebrate Christmas with all its traditions, family gatherings, and goodwill unto others!

"Suddenly a great army of heaven's angels appeared, singing praises to God: Glory to God in the highest heaven, and peace on earth to those with whom he is pleased!

The shepherds said to one another, 'Let's go to Bethlehem and see this thing that has happened, which the Lord has told us.'"

~The Gospel according to Luke

"I serve my parish by preaching, teaching, healing... I try to convey the love and compassion of God in Jesus Christ for all people, and the fellowship with God, and with one another."

~Fr. Michael Ruane

The afternoon sun and Nativity, St. Michael's Catholic Church, Poplar Springs; 2007

Saint Michael is one of the three Archangels, and is the leader of the celestial ranks and the conqueror of Satan. He is depicted usually as a warrior, often holding scales. His name in Hebrew means, "Who is like God," and he is the protector of grocers, paratroopers, and the police.

St. Michael's Catholic Church, in Poplar Springs, was founded in 1879. On June 12, 1880, the corner stone for St. Michael's Catholic Church and cemetery was laid on the grounds donated by Mr. Kuhn. The first Mass in the church was celebrated by Reverend Edward I. Devitt, who became the church's regular pastor three years later.

In 1956, St. Michael's celebrated its 75th jubilee, and was honored by the presence of His Excellency Francis P. Keough, Archbishop of Baltimore. In 1964, after 82 years of being a mission church, His Eminence Lawrence Cardinal Sheehan, the Archbishop of Baltimore at the time, established St. Michael's as a parish church. In 1979, St. Michael's celebrated its 100th Anniversary.

In 1966, a parish rectory was built on land purchased from Mr. Triplet. Soon after, in 1974, a new multi-purpose building was erected. A new church was added in 1982, and the ground-breaking ceremony was celebrated by Bishop P. Francis Murphy.

The present parish priest, Reverend Father Michael J. Ruane, was appointed in December, 1988. Father Michael serves his parish by preaching, teaching, healing, and administrating church duties. He tries to convey the love and compassion of God in Jesus Christ for all people, and the fellowship with God, and with one another.

Father Michael has 1579 households in his congregation, coming from Howard, Carroll, Montgomery, and Frederick counties. He has over 500 volunteers involved in ministries of the church.

The Social Service Committee, of the Pastoral Council, reaches out to the community through the Food Cellar, St. Vincent Mobile Clothing Bank, Red Cross Blood Drive, Pastoral Visitors to Homebound and Nursing Homes, Youth Ministry Lunches to Beacon House in Frederick County, and Beans & Bread in Baltimore City.

The church's 125th Anniversary was celebrated in 2004. This celebration coincided with the renovation and building of the new Religious Education Wing and Multi-purpose Building. The celebratory event was an inspiration to Fr. Michael and his congregation, as it was a major milestone in the church and community.

Milestones are easy to spot in this neck of the woods, as much of the area is pristine, with wide open fields of corn, wheat, and cattle pasture. For the truly religious, this is where one would want to come to pray, as God's creation is visible for miles.

I will never forget that I found Christmas in a Nativity scene in Poplar Springs.

Northern Howard County

The B&O Railroad Museum, Ellicott City; Mt. Hebron Presbyterian Church, Ellicott City; St. John's Episcopal Church, Ellicott City; Epiphany Lutheran Church, Ellicott City; 2009

Howard's Northeastern view is Baltimore
Where baseball's Babe Ruth is held aglow
Holy Fathers came from over there to here
To preach the Sacred Words still held dear

    Northern Howard County encompasses parts of West Friendship and Sykesville (in the Northwest), Marriottsville, Woodstock, and parts of Ellicott City (in the Northeast). This region is bounded by Carroll County to the Northwest, and Baltimore County to the Northeast.

    At the Northwestern end, I discovered that St. Barnabas Episcopal Church was located in Sykesville, Howard County, but that its office building was located on busy Main Street, just inside the Carroll County border. Much of this region is rural, and farming is still the main livelihood for many.

    At the Northeastern end, farming was the main livelihood, since the 1700s, in Old Town Ellicott City. Ellicott City was founded by the three Ellicott brothers (John, Andrew, and Joseph) who came from Buck's County, Pennsylvania. The Ellicott brothers persuaded the local farmers to grow wheat instead of tobacco, and thereby, the brothers began a prosperous milling town. Being of the Quaker faith themselves, they believed in hard work and prayer to God. They were also open-minded to members of other denominations, who sought to buy land from them for their own churches.

    Today, Old Town Ellicott City is a bustling little town where numerous antique shops, fine restaurants, and churches have replaced the farms and mills. The town, over the centuries, has acquired a long history, and much of it can be found in Howard County's first Catholic Church, St. Paul's.

    Right between West Friendship and Ellicott City is Marriottsville. This is where the Bon Secours Spiritual Life Center is located. The Bon Secours campus is over 300 acres, and the Stone House on the property was the original house that came with the acquisition. At first sight, it would appear that not a whole lot goes on at this secluded retreat. But, upon further exploration, there is much retreating, learning, and praying that goes on at this center. I was fortunate to be able to paint their beautiful landscape and Stone House.

    The churches that I have represented in this section with paintings, photographs, interviews, and history include St. Barnabas Episcopal Church, Sykesville; Bon Secours Spiritual Life Center, Marriottsville; and St. Paul's Catholic Church, in Old Town Ellicott City. Places and churches that I have represented with just photographs include the B&O Railroad Museum, Main Street, Mt. Hebron Presbyterian Church, St. John's Episcopal Church, and Epiphany Lutheran Church, all located in Ellicott City.

"Reflected Passion" 24"x24" o/c; March 2008

"REFLECTED PASSION"

(St. Barnabas Episcopal Church, Sykesville)

When I first considered St. Barnabas Episcopal Church, Sykesville, as my next subject to paint, it was December, 2007. I was hoping to do a "snowy" painting, but there was no snow. In January, 2008, we had a little snow and ice, but various diversions, like a three-week visit by my sister, kept me from painting. My sister Deepthi and I spent much time baking, collaging, and playing the piano.

Another constant in an artist's world is the cost of supplies. It had been almost three months since my supply source had had a good sale. I kept checking their website, and when I had reached my wits end, I decided to ask them when the next sale would be. Well, the very next day, my hopes were fulfilled, and I was reminded of the phrase from the Bible, "Ask, and thou shall receive." Although my request was menial in comparison to what most would ask the Lord, I felt that my little world was alive, again. I could now paint St. Barnabas Episcopal Church!

So, I arrived on March 18, 2008, at St. Barnabas. The church was tucked away atop a hill within the Howard County border, on Forsythe Road in Sykesville. Though it was sunny, the chill in the air inspired me to paint the front of the church in an icy, blue-white. The stone building and its setting conveyed a feeling of "Old English."

Since it was Holy Week, there was a great cross, draped with a purple shroud, set outside in the parking lot. The shroud was symbolic of Christ's robes during His Passion. The shadow, that the cross cast on the parking lot, became an interesting compositional element. As I painted, I was reminded of Christ's final journey through Jerusalem and His death on Good Friday.

Since my knowledge of Christian denominations was limited, the good Reverend Earl Mullins, rector of St. Barnabas, gave me the best explanation one could get. According to Reverend Mullins, Christianity has three major Constellations: Catholics, whose primary source of authority is Tradition (what the Church believes God has revealed to it since the time of Christ); Protestants, whose primary source of authority is the Bible - in a relatively literal way; and Anglicans, whose sources of authority are like a balanced three-legged stool, composed of Tradition, Scripture, and Reason.

The Episcopal Church is an independent province within the worldwide Anglican Communion. The symbolic "see" or seat is presided by the Archbishop of Canterbury, who lives in Lambeth Palace, London. The governing body within a parish church is called a Vestry. The Episcopalian Church is open, tolerant, and inclusive of differences. Their teachings accept the theory of evolution as well as life styles and orientations that are not readily accepted in many other denominations.

Reverend Mullins was very enthused by the newly elected first African-American Episcopal Bishop of Maryland, the Rt. Reverend Eugene Sutton. Mullins said that each diocese has a bishop who is elected by clergy and lay representatives, from all the parishes within a particular diocese.

"...Because there is the one loaf of bread, all of us, though many, are one body, for we all share the same loaf..."

~First Letter from Paul to the Corinthians

"The Episcopalian Mass has more Scripture readings than most...the first reading is from the Hebrew Scripture. The second reading is usually a Psalm, the third is an Epistle - letters from St. Paul, and the last is from one of the four Gospels..."

~Fr. Earl Mullins

St. Barnabas Episcopal Church, Sykesville; 2008
Chefs at the St. Barnabas "Shrove Tuesday" celebration; 2009

St. Barnabas Holy Trinity Parish was founded in 1771, as a Colonial parish in Carroll County. St. Barnabas Church on Forsythe Road, Howard County, was built in 1850, as a "chapel of ease" for those who could not make the journey to Carroll County. But soon, St. Barnabas became the parish church, and the church in Carroll County was closed and incorporated by St. Barnabas in Howard County.

The mission of St. Barnabas is, "To become more like Jesus Christ, reaching out to the community, empowering Youth with the Christian compassion and wisdom of Seniors and empowering Seniors with the love and energy of the Youth." As the church's pastor, Reverend W. Earl Mullins strives to live his church's mission on a daily basis. When I went to the church office to interview him, he took the time to thank and appreciate the lady who did the cleaning of the office and church buildings.

Father Mullins previously served as rector of historic St. Paul's Church in Dedham, Massachusetts. His parish there was around 500 members. At St. Barnabas, he has served as the rector for nine years. The original size, when he arrived, was about 60 members, which has since tripled in his time. The average family is middle class, and the church is very inclusive. Parishioners come from the immediate surroundings, and from as far as Westminster, Glen Burnie, Ellicott City, and Columbia, Maryland. His first Mass here was on Easter Sunday, 2000. At St. Barnabas, he celebrates three Masses on Sundays, with the 8:00 a.m. Mass being a traditional Rite 1 spoken service; the 9:15 a.m. one being more contemporary; and the 11:15 a.m. being a traditional sung service. At 10:30 a.m., religious educational classes are held.

Father Mullins took the time to educate me in some of the differences between Episcopalian and other Christian denominations. One difference was that the Episcopalian Mass had more Scripture readings than most. They honored their Judea-Christian roots with the first reading from the Hebrew Scripture. Their second reading was usually a Psalm, the third was an Epistle - letter from St. Paul, and the last reading was from one of the four Gospels according to Matthew, Mark, Luke or John.

The biggest influence that this parish has had as a community is in the area of outreach. After Hurricane Katrina hit in 2005, St. Barnabas sent three teams to rebuild houses and devastated communities in New Orleans. For the victims, the parishioners collected and delivered five truck-loads of food, personal and household items. Locally, they work in conjunction with the Salvation Army and the "Feed More" van that delivers food to those who call the streets "home" in Baltimore, Maryland. They also have outreach ministries with Springfield Hospital, the Sykesville Girls Shelter, and much more. Since the congregation has grown, one of their long-term goals is to build a new parish hall.

Of the many community social events that take place at St. Barnabas, Rev. Mullins recalled their annual "Shrove Tuesday" celebration as being the most significant. This grand breakfast celebration includes large helpings of country sausage, eggs, and blueberry & apple pancakes. Large crowds usually attend this event. On Shrove Tuesday, February 24, 2009, I experienced not only the warmth and generosity of this congregation, but also the style and ambiance of a delicious breakfast!

I will never forget the shadow cast by the cross at St. Barnabas - a shadow of rebirth?

"A Spiritual Walk" 30"x30" o/c; March 2008

"A SPIRITUAL WALK"

(Bon Secours Spiritual Life Center, Marriottsville)

Painting anything during early Spring was always a joy. It was March, 2008, and Spring had just begun. The birds were chirping, and the trees were starting to blossom. Where would I go next? My curiosity brought me to Bon Secours Spiritual Life Center in Marriottsville, Maryland.

I arrived at the campus and began to look around. I was considering painting the Provincial House that included the chapel, but I was not inspired by the architecture or the little light that shone on it, as it was surrounded by trees. So, I looked further, and the Stone House caught my eye. Although the center does not conduct any religious services in the house, many meetings and spiritual activities are held here.

The Stone House was the original residence of the owner of this magnificat estate of 313 acres of wooded and farm land. The Stone House was acquired by the Sisters of Bon Secours in conjunction with the land purchase. The house is now used as a learning and meeting center for the Health System offices.

As I spent four days painting on this campus, I was inspired daily by the types of conversations that I usually did not encounter. A pastor walked by me on his way to the chapel where Mass is celebrated at 11:00 a.m. every morning. He said, "May you be blessed in your beautiful talent." Wow, I always knew that I experienced a Divine connection with the Lord whenever I painted, but to be blessed for it made me feel very special. Another conversation among two women went something like this: "I never knew how inter-connected religion and spirituality were," said one lady. The other replied, "They are one and the same." My reflection at that moment was, that no matter what denomination, spirituality always gets us through our challenges in the real world.

At that moment of reflection, I suddenly experienced the brightest of light that shone on the side of the Stone House right at 11:30 a.m., and then, that light illuminated the newly blooming tulip blossoms on the tulip tree across the walkway. These blossoms soon became a million points of light that illuminated my path through life's journey.

Of the illuminated, is Dr. Thomas Little, executive director of Bon Secours Spiritual Life Center, who has a background in theology, and has been coming to the center since 1971, for retreats. "Bon Secours hosts many annual retreats and days of prayer. The center provides services to the religious, and to persons who want to deepen their spirituality," said Dr. Little. The center serves groups from Maryland, Virginia, West Virginia, and Delaware. Churches and other organizations bring their councils, leadership groups, and their congregations for various retreats at Bon Secours.

Bon Secours Spiritual Life Center campus, Marriottsville; 2008

The Provincial House (which is shaped like a cross) was founded in 1965, by the Sisters of Bon Secours ("Good Help" in French), who were originally formed in 1824, in Paris, France. The sisters were invited to the United States by Cardinal Gibbons, to help provide healthcare for the poor and the sick in Baltimore, where the first house was established. In the early 1960s, the sisters decided to expand, and established the Provincial House in Marriottsville, Maryland, in 1965. The primary goal of the center is to practice ways to grow closer to God, and to be good partners with area churches.

The Provincial House is home to the offices, and the chapel in which daily Mass and a variety of liturgical services are offered. Within the Provincial House is Marian Hall, a home for the retired sisters. Farther away from the Stone House is another building, built in 1983, that is home to the National Office of the Bon Secours Health System, Inc. The sisters run the health system here. The employees collect food and supplies which they donate to families and groups in Baltimore and Howard Counties. As it celebrates its 40th year, Bon Secours continues to serve the church and community.

In the near future, the center hopes to develop more trails and walking areas. Of the paths already in existence, the Labyrinth is of significance. It was built in February, 1999, and is the focal point of a one-acre "sacred space," set aside as the Holy Ground, to commemorate the 175th Anniversary of the founding of the Congregation of Bon Secours of Paris.

"The Labyrinth is a symbolic pilgrimage journey to the Divine. It is based on the design of the Chartres Labyrinth, laid in the floor of the Chartres Cathedral around 1220, in Paris. Unlike a maze, the Labyrinth has only one path which leads to the center and out again. The path winds throughout, and becomes a mirror for where we are in our lives; it touches our sorrow and releases our joys," explains the center's brochure.

On two occasions, I walked the Labyrinth at Bon Secours. My personal experience was that it gave me a chance to reflect on the moment, on my personal life, and God's precious gifts by which we are surrounded. Walking in it made me slow down my daily pace and breathe deeply the crisp air and take in the stones, the moss, the leaves, and the Spring day.

Labyrinth at Bon Secours, Marriottsville; 2008

Provincial House at Bon Secours Spiritual Life Center, Marriottsville; 2008

The philosophy of the Sisters of Bon Secours is rooted in their call from God and their mission in the Roman Catholic Church, to help bring people to wholeness, to alleviate human suffering, and to help others experience a deeper awareness of their own spirituality.

There are approximately 400 Sisters of Bon Secours serving the Church in five provinces, located in Great Britain, Ireland, France, Peru, and the United States. As of January, 2009, the Congregation removed its provincial boundaries, and began a new leadership model. During February, 2008, approximately 140 sisters came from around the world to Marriottsville (the United States headquarters), to formulate their new model. They called their gathering "Come With Hope."

Many people come with the hopes of finding and renewing themselves when they attend a retreat. Retreat services provide a variety of experiences and offer creative opportunities with gifted national and local presenters. Both individual and group opportunities await for those seeking to deepen their relationship with God.

So, what kind of seminars and retreats does Bon Secours have to offer? In looking at their calendar, I found things for every walk of life. On their calendar of events for 2008, one could visit several exhibitions that included a "Blessed Union of Souls," "Quilts - Art to Help Mend the World," and "Photography by the Provincial House, Spiritual Center & Health System co-workers." There were book-signing events, and a Celtic Spirituality retreat, concert, and open house. The year's calendar ended with Brunch with Santa, and a family Advent concert, reception and tours.

Many of the retreats were focused around a central theme. In the silent retreat entitled, "Friends' Day of Prayer," participants met with a spiritual director, daily, to reflect on God's presence and movement in their life, and to deepen their awareness and response to God. In a guided retreat entitled, "Living The Peace Prayer of St. Francis," participants were urged to go deep into the heart of Gospel love, embracing every relationship with a spirit of integrity and compassion.

Of course, I almost jumped out of my skin when I discovered among the long list of retreats, one that was entitled, "Art and Spirituality: Nourishing Your Connection with Art, Spirit and Meaning." The registration fee included lunch and art supplies. In the description, I found out that it was a day for one to enter the river where spirit, art, and meaning became one; the river from which artworks could be created. The retreat promised a day of playing, making, learning, reflecting, and responding. Although I did not attend that retreat, I knew that I would have enjoyed it, as this was what my purpose has been during the past two years: to find spirituality along my painting and writing journey of the churches in Howard County, Maryland!

I will never forget letting my worries untangle along the Labyrinth at Bon Secours.

"St. Paul In The City" 36"x36" o/c; April 2008

"ST. PAUL IN THE CITY"

(St. Paul's Catholic Church, Ellicott City)

After my experiences at Bon Secours, I felt that I had connected completely with the Divine, and that I was wearing a Halo above my head. I felt that myself and the world had changed for the better, and that everyone I was around was "blessed" in what they did. So, my next destination was Old Town, Ellicott City. As I arrived one April afternoon (2008), the town was bustling with everyday city life - from vendors on the sidewalks to delivery trucks parked in the middle of the street, to elegant restaurants alongside not so elegant places. I parked my SUV in a designated parking lot (that was metered) and had to carry my heavy easel (now on its very last legs), canvas (36" x 36"), and supply bag, from Main Street uphill to St. Paul's Street. As I walked by the historic Baltimore & Ohio Railroad Museum, I was approached by a man driving an SUV who swung in to talk to me. He said that he was a fellow artist, and commiserated with me over my weathered easel. I was touched by his interest, but then he proceeded to invite me to visit his gallery, when I was done with painting for the day. Though flattered by the invitation, I steered him away by letting him know that I had to pick up my son from school. I was certainly not inspired by the suggestiveness of his invitation, but kept on my way, with my Halo above my head, and the Lord watching over me.

As I reached St. Paul's Catholic church at the top of the hill, I looked up with wonder at this setting. Here, on a narrow road on top of a hill, stood a church that seemed to balance itself between the heavens above and the good, the bad, and the ugly down below - with only a stone wall to separate them. I kept my focus on the church as I worked, because the activity below was not limited to noise and smog, but also to consistent unwanted attention from passers-by.

The light and air were crisp, and Spring was in full bloom. As I started to paint, I realized that this was the last painting in my series, and I painted with full heart and soul, not only to capture the light at the given window of 2:00-3:00 p.m., but also to capture the Divine Spirit that seemed to bathe over me one last time. One afternoon, I became aware that the Lord was with me again, because an elderly gentleman walked by, and stopped to admire my painting. He happened to mention that he, too, was a writer, and that he was exploring his Scottish roots. He also mentioned that he had played a part in the TV mini-series, "John Adams." I was tickled at my brush with a famous TV star!

St. Paul's is no stranger to the famous. The famous baseball player, Babe Ruth, was married in this church on October 14, 1914. He was one of the most prominent individuals married here. Many of the church's founding families were baptized, wedded and memorialized here, too. Life-long church member, Mr. Jim Lilly, mentioned to a newspaper reporter that his grandparents were among the founding families of St. Paul's, which was erected in 1838, and was the first Catholic Church between Baltimore and Frederick.

The altar at St. Paul's Catholic Church; 2008

Howard County used to be part of Anne Arundel County, in an area known as "West Ilchester." Howard became a separate county in 1851. At the county's Northeastern end is Ellicott City, home to St. Paul's Roman Catholic Church. St. Paul's was built of gray granite on land purchased from the Ellicotts for $5.00. It was completed in 1838, and dedicated on December 13, of that year, by Archbishop Eccleston. The bell was placed in the tower in 1844, and weighed 555 pounds. In 1896, the church steeple was built to its present height, about 100 feet above the ground. According to the baptismal registry between 1839-1858, there were only four Catholics residing in the town during the early 1800s: an Irishman, a German, an American, and an African.

The first pastor, Father Coskery, was instrumental in bringing the Christian Brothers to the United States. The Christian Brothers bought Rock Hill Academy in 1857, and they re-named it Rock Hill College. Sadly, the college burned down in 1923.

Before the construction of St. Paul's Rectory in 1844, the pastors of St. Paul's resided in the Castle Angelo, a large brown shingle building. At that time, some worshiped in this building, and at other times, in the chapel at Doughoregan Manor. Among the notable family names found in the marriage and baptismal registries, from the mid 1800s, are families whose present generations still live in the vicinity. They are the Owings, the Lillys, the Cecils, the Dorseys, the Clarks, the Gaithers, the Hardings, the Whites, the Ellicotts, the Warfields, the MacTavishs, and the Carrolls.

Under the direction of Monsignor Ryan, in 1922, the old Patapsco National Bank building was converted into a Grammar School (during segregation) for the white children. Msgr. Ryan also established a two-room school for the colored children, in a building that had been used as a hall and Sunday school room. Among the children attending were of the staff from Doughoregan Manor, home of Charles Carroll, signer of the Declaration of Independence. St. Paul's has been described by many as a "gem in an exquisite setting." Prior pastor Father Michael Jendrek once stated, "St. Paul's is a beautiful worship environment combined with a welcoming community."

Painting this tall, narrow church tower and adjoining buildings, that sat atop a hill on a winding road, was not easy. Keeping the proportions accurate was a feat, as I had to gauge verticality of the original tower against the angular distortions of the walkway and railing in the foreground. The surface of the tower, too, presented challenges not only for the stone, but also for the carvings and ornamentation that embellished it.

Of the many architectural features of a church, I have always had a soft spot for stained-glass windows as seen in the sanctuary of St. Paul's. The originator of the Gothic style, Abbot Suger, of the Royal Abbey of St. Denis, France, said this about stained-glass windows, "...the 'miraculous' light flooding the choir through the 'most sacred' windows becomes the 'Light Divine', a mystic revelation of the Spirit of God."

Stained-glass window in St. Paul's Catholic Church; 2008

Entrance to St. Paul's Catholic Church, Ellicott City; 2008

A sermon during Mass is often not only a reflection of what the Gospel reading was about, but also, it is the relationship between what was read and the needs in our daily lives. A memorable sermon, most frequently, is defined by how well the pastor delivers this relationship with personal experiences and interesting stories. A good delivery with a few jokes always keeps the congregation awake, too. During my visit to St. Paul's for Mass on Sunday, August 2, 2008, I had to applaud Father Matthew Buening for an exceptional sermon. The Gospel had been about the miracle of the fishes and the loaves of bread - a story that I had learned in childhood. When I first heard the beginning of it, I thought, "this is nothing new - I think I'll let my mind wander for this one." But, Father Matt had my attention from the moment he brought in his personal experience, while visiting the Naval Academy in Annapolis, Maryland. He narrated how he was asked to pass the salt at a meal there, and how he generously helped himself to it, before passing it on. According to Naval code, one could be expelled for such an act. The code states that one has to serve others before oneself, just as the Lord served the fishes and loaves to the hungry before he thought of Himself.

So, after his warm and gregarious sermon, I decided I had to talk to Father Matthew Tobias Buening in person. I introduced myself, and was delighted that he would grant me an interview.

Aside from sharing with me the mission of his church and their charities (PATH and St. Vincent de Paul), Father Matt wanted to share his generosity by presenting me with a copy of the book entitled, *St. Paul's Church and Parish*, by the late Brother Fabrician. This book was published on November 4, 1910 - almost a hundred years ago. It included details about the Patapsco Female Institute and Rock Hill College, which today are in ruin and preserved for historical benefit. Aside from the history associated with the church, the descriptions of everyday life in this book were also quite charming.

Brother Fabrician's book, told in story-format, gave vivid descriptions of church events such as the annual picnic held on the 4th of July, or on Lady Day in August. The conversations surrounding the main dishes, during the meal, went somewhat like this: "Won't you have a piece of my tongue, Father Dougherty?" asked Mrs. Crowley. To which Mr. Crowley replied, "Thank God Father, she's going to cut a piece of it off...we'll have peace in the house after this." Speaking of food, at the Historical Society I came across a menu from the church's Centennial Dinner held in October, 1938. For appetizers: Fruit Cocktail, Sweet Gherkin, Queen Olives, Hearts of Celery, and Consomme Madrenal. For the main course: Roast Young Turkey, Cranberry Jelly, Candied Sweet Potatoes, Creamed Hominy, and Sauerkraut. For dessert: Ice Cream and Cakes. What a scrumptious spread!

Spreading the Word of God was Saint Paul the Apostle's mission. He participated in Christian persecutions until he had a vision that led him to convert. He is known as the protector of theologians and the Catholic press. His name is Latin for "humble."

It was with humble brush-strokes that I completed "St. Paul In The City" and this chapter in my life.

I will never forget the old-world charms within St. Paul's and Historic Ellicott City.

Main Street in Old Town, Ellicott City; 2008

CONCLUSION

Tuesday, February 24, 2009 was Shrove Tuesday or Fat Tuesday, and I found myself in church reflecting on the day. This was the day before Lent. Lent represents the forty days that Christ spent fasting and praying. It has been a complete two years since I began this project, and I am fulfilled.

The fourteen paintings through Howard County, Maryland, were done within fourteen months to symbolize the fourteen Stations of the Cross. Each painting was a challenge in itself - trying to compose on a cross-shaped canvas, and trying to depict my subjects in black, white, and four shades of gray. My goal was to capture the nuances of light and dark, intensity, and texture, with these basic six colors. Artistically, I feel accomplished for trying something I had never tried before.

Throughout my research, I found many common threads among the churches, even though each denomination had a different doctrine, hierarchy, and rituals. In common, each denomination preached the teachings of a superior being, each encouraged their believers to live in peace and harmony with the world, each promoted goodwill to others through community service projects, and each taught that much could be accomplished through strong and collective faith.

During my research, I have to say that I found each church to be a treasure-trove of historic information. I tip my hat to the historians who have spent painstaking hours archiving their church history. The pastors and priests, too, were amazing, for their Divine inspirations and earthly experiences.

I also discovered that earthly experiences and Divine inspirations were not limited just to the clergy. Along the way, I attended a seminar by a famous chemistry professor - Dr. Lothar Schafer - whose presentation was entitled, "Non-Empirical Reality: Transcending the Physical and the Spiritual in the Order of the One." Dr. Schafer sought to connect his earthly chemical findings with the Divine. What further inspired me was his experience at Chartres Cathedral, my favorite Gothic church in France. Schafer said, "Once I was sitting in the Cathedral of Chartres. All of a sudden, the thought crossed my mind that, at one time, the Cosmic Spirit had burst out of the ground there and cast itself into stone. In places like this, the feeling of a transcendent presence can be overwhelming." I experienced the same while painting and writing about each of these fourteen churches in Howard County, MD.

All throughout this journey, I have gained a new perspective on why we need church in our lives. It is more than just going to Mass on Sundays or doing the occasional charitable act. Church is something that shapes our lives, and it is what we often turn to if we are carrying a daily cross.

As we all bear our crosses in life, my hope is that my parents' cross, with regard to my sister, will someday become less burdensome. Perhaps if her illness continues after my parents are gone, I would pick up that same cross and carry it through. Having experienced the various denominations and their teachings while writing this book, I believe that in the future, I could carry that cross to wherever it takes me. I believe that the Good Lord will guide me though the challenges ahead, and that for all those who face such challenges, that He may be with them every step of the way!

"Be merciful to me, Lord and restore my health...You will help me, because I do what is right; you will keep me in your presence forever."

~Psalm 41

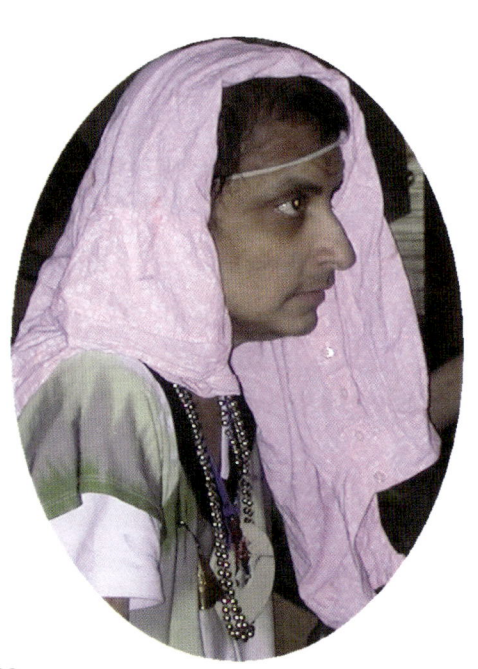

"God is our shelter and strength, always ready to help in times of trouble. So we will not be afraid, even if the earth is shaken and mountains fall into the ocean depths..."

~Psalm 46

Stained-glass window in St. Michael's, Poplar Springs; 2008
My Sister, Deepthi Codippily, at my home; 2009

SOURCES OF INFORMATION & INSPIRATION

PAGE 8	*The King James Holy Bible,* T. Nelson, 1987; Howard County landscape; H.C. Economic Development Authority (www.hceda.org); www.en.wikipedia.org.
PAGE 9	*History of Art* by H.W. Janson, Prentice Hall, Inc. NJ, 1977; *Michelangelo and The Pope's Ceiling* by Ross King, Penguin Books, 2003; *The Abstract Expressionists* by E.V. Thaw, The Metropolitan MOA, 1987.
PAGE 11	www.en.wikipedia.org.
PAGE 13-15	Interview with Father John Burkhard; Inspirations from Sr. Catherine, Mr. K. Rickbeil and Mr. T. McCormick; *King James Holy Bible*, T. Nelson, 1987; "A Celebration of Corpus Christi Chapel" booklet.
PAGE 17-19	Interview with Pastor Leslie Metcalf; "History of Melville Methodist Church" documentation by J. Edward Head; www.en.wikipedia.org.
PAGE 21-25	Interview with Rev. Father Bowen; *History of Art* by H.W. Janson, Prentice Hall, Inc. NJ, 1977; *Michelangelo and The Pope's Ceiling* by Ross King, Penguin Books, 2003; "S.A.C.C. Parish Handbook".
PAGE 27	Interview with Will Iager; www.nps.gov; www.savagemill.org.
PAGE 29-31	Interview with Pastor Robinson; CFC pamphlets; *The International Student Bible*, T. Nelson, 1999. *The Vatican* by F. Papafava, SCALA 1984; *History of Art* by H.W. Janson, Prentice Hall, Inc. NJ, 1977.
PAGE 33-37	Interview with Will Iager; "About Being Lutheran" booklet, Channing Bete Company, Inc., 1974; www.stpaulfulton.org; *Saints, A Year In Faith And Art* by Rosa Giorgi, Harry N. Abrams, Inc. NY, 2006.
PAGE 39-43	Interview with Msgr. Luca; Interview with Mr. Art Boone; *Saints, A Year In Faith And Art* by Rosa Giorgi, Harry N. Abrams, Inc. NY, 2006; "S.L.P. Directory", 2007; picnic attendees.
PAGE 45	www.columbia.com; www.beth-shalom.net; www.datweb.blogspot.com.
PAGE 47-51	Interview with Father Noel Danielewicz; "Faith At Folly Quarter" by Companions of St. Anthony, www.companionsofstanthony.org; *Theories Of Modern Art* by H. B. Chipp, University of California Press, 1968; www.wikipedia.org.
PAGE 53	Glenelg United Methodist Church Directory; "Churches Which Are No More," *The Times, E.C. MD,* 1965.
PAGE 55-57	Interview with Pastor Jerry Cooper; *History of Art* by H.W. Janson, Prentice Hall, Inc. NJ, 1977; www.walnutsprings.com; www.historicec.com.
PAGE 59-61	"History of St. Andrew's" documentation by Cynthia McNaughten, Louanne Sargent, and the late Marguerite Sargent; *Saints, A Year In Faith And Art* by Rosa Giorgi, Harry N. Abrams, Inc. NY, 2006.
PAGE 63-67	Interview with Rev. Dr. Lisa Bandel-Sparks; "History of LUMC" documentation by and interview with Mrs. Martha Embrey; the community at the Lisbon Firehouse.
PAGE 69-71	Interview with Father Michael Ruane; www.stmichaelspoplarsprings.org; *Saints, A Year In Faith And Art* by Rosa Giorgi, Harry N. Abrams,Inc. NY, 2006.
PAGE 73	www.enwikipedia.org.
PAGE 75-77	Interview with Rev. Earl Mullins; "St. Barnabas" newsletter, November 2008.
PAGE 79-83	Interview with Executive Director Dr. Thomas E. Little; "Bridges" booklet edited by B. Castellano, 2008; "Focus" booklet by the Sisters of Bon Secours, 2008; Retreat and Conference Center pamphlet.
PAGE 85-89	Interview with Fr. Matthew Tobias Buening; *St. Paul's Church and Parish, E.C. MD* by Brother Fabrician, Foley Brothers, Baltimore, MD, 1910; "St. Paul's in H.C. Rich in Tradition," *The Catholic Review*; "Oldest Parish in H.C. Gets Younger," *The Catholic Review*, 2005, "St. Paul's Celebrates 160 Years, " *Ellicott City 21043*, 1998; "St. Paul's Lived The Town's History," *The Times, Ellicott City, MD,* 1985; St. Paul's Catholic Church Centennial Dinner Menu, 1938; "St Paul's Church History" by Church Historians; *Saints, A Year In Faith And Art* by Rosa Giorgi, Harry N. Abrams, Inc. NY, 2006.
PAGE 91	"Non-Empirical Reality" presentation by Dr. Lothar Schafer, University of Arkansas, AR, 2007.

LOCATION OF PAINTING SITES & CHURCHES

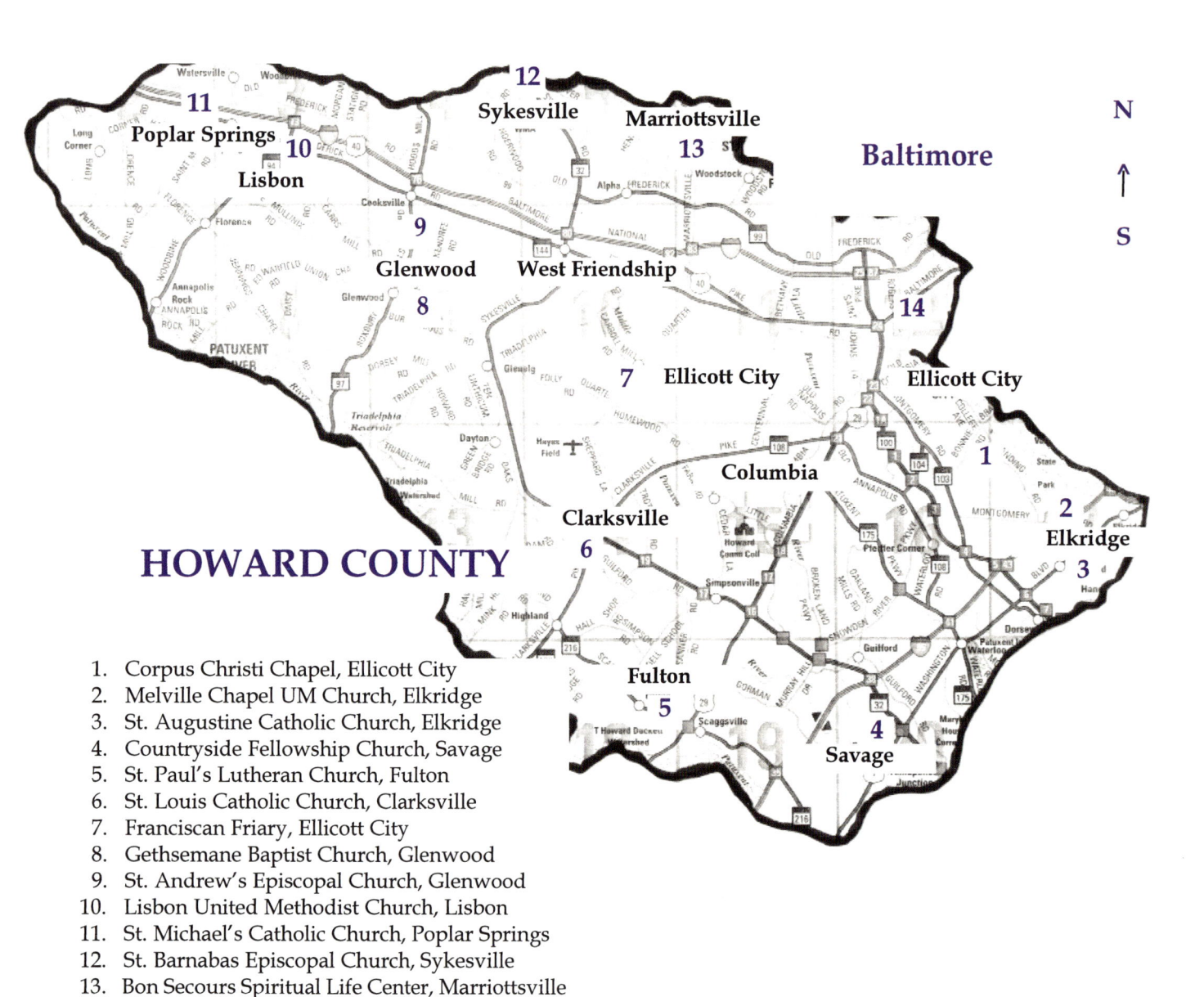

HOWARD COUNTY

Baltimore

Washington, D.C.

1. Corpus Christi Chapel, Ellicott City
2. Melville Chapel UM Church, Elkridge
3. St. Augustine Catholic Church, Elkridge
4. Countryside Fellowship Church, Savage
5. St. Paul's Lutheran Church, Fulton
6. St. Louis Catholic Church, Clarksville
7. Franciscan Friary, Ellicott City
8. Gethsemane Baptist Church, Glenwood
9. St. Andrew's Episcopal Church, Glenwood
10. Lisbon United Methodist Church, Lisbon
11. St. Michael's Catholic Church, Poplar Springs
12. St. Barnabas Episcopal Church, Sykesville
13. Bon Secours Spiritual Life Center, Marriottsville
14. St. Paul's Catholic Church, Ellicott City

CURRENT NEWSPAPER HEADLINES

ABOUT THE AUTHOR

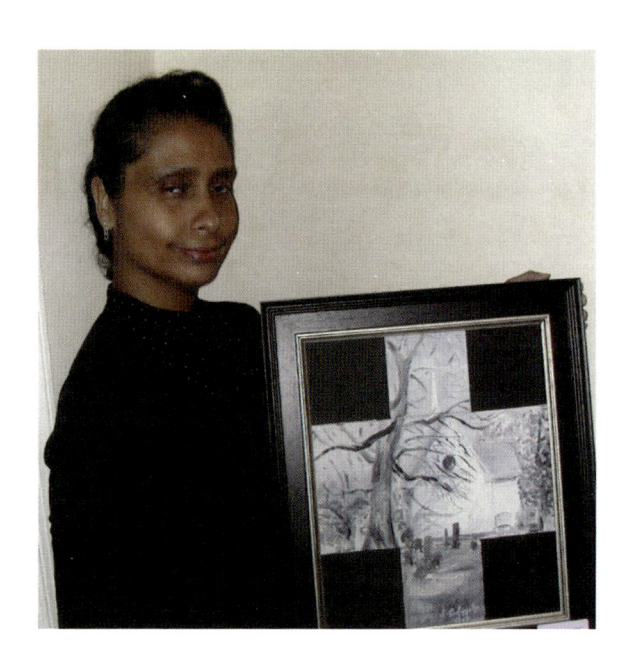

Shyami Codippily was born in Colombo, Sri Lanka in 1966. She moved to the United States in 1981, and currently lives in West Friendship, Maryland, with her husband Scott Murphy, son Taylor, and Golden Retriever Polo.

She attended Walt Whitman High School in Bethesda, Maryland, Carnegie-Mellon University in Pittsburgh, Pennsylvania, and the University of Maryland in College Park, Maryland. She graduated with a B.A. degree, majoring in Fine Art and minoring in Art History.

Her awards include the UNICEF International Art Award, 1979, and was honored as one of the Top Twenty Artists in the United States, 1985, by the National Foundation For the Arts. She enjoys painting in oil and gouache, and sculpting in marble and quartz. Her paintings and other works have been displayed in various locations, and have been widely collected. She is also the author of *Farms Never To Be Forgotten* - an artistic and literary journey that explores the farms in Howard County, Maryland.

The "Churches Never To Be Forgotten" collection of paintings was first exhibited at St. Paul's Catholic Church in Ellicott City, Maryland, during the 2009 Easter season. Since then, the collection has traveled to several venues, including the Manor House at the Franciscan Friary, in Ellicott City, Maryland, and has received much recognition.

Aside from spending time with her family and friends, she enjoys serving her community. She is a lector at Trinity's Corpus Christi Chapel, Ellicott City, and she volunteers for several organizations.

Made in the USA